By 10/6

GLADSTONE

and

Liberalism

is one of the volumes
in the
TEACH YOURSELF HISTORY
LIBRARY

Teach Yourself History

VOLUMES READY OR IN PREPARATION

The Use of History, by A. L. Rowse
Pericles and Athens, by A. R. Burn
Alexander the Great and the Hellenistic Empire, by A. R. Burn
Agricola and Roman Britain, by A. R. Burn
Charlemagne and Western Europe, by H. St. L. B. Moss
Constantine and the Conversion of Europe, by A. H. M. Jones
Wycliffe and the Beginnings of English Nonconformity, by K. B. McFarlane
Henry V and the Invasion of France, by E. F. Jacob
Joan of Arc and the Recovery of France, by Alice Buchan
Lorenzo dei Medici and Renaissance Italy, by C. N. Ady
Machiavelli and Renaissance Italy by John Hale
Erasmus and the Northern Renaissance, by Margaret Mann Phillips
Thomas Cromwell and the English Reformation, by A. G. Dickens
Cranmer and the English Reformation, by F. E. Hutchinson
Elizabeth I and the Unity of England, by J. Hurstfield
Whitgift and the English Church, by V. J. K. Brook
Raleigh and the British Empire, by D. B. Quinn
Richelieu and the French Monarchy, by C. V. Wedgwood
Oliver Cromwell and the Puritan Revolution, by Maurice Ashley
Milton and the English Mind, by F. E. Hutchinson
Louis XIV and the Greatness of France, by Maurice Ashley
Peter the Great and the Emergence of Russia, by B. H. Sumner
Chatham and the British Empire, by Sir Charles Grant Robertson
Cook and the Opening of the Pacific, by James A. Williamson
Catherine the Great and the Expansion of Russia, by Gladys Scott Thomson
Benjamin Franklin and the American People, by Esmond Wright
Warren Hastings and British India, by Penderel Moon
Washington and the American Revolution, by Esmond Wright
Robespierre and the French Revolution, by J. M. Thompson
Napoleon and the Awakening of Europe, by Felix Markham
Bolivar and the Independence of Spanish America, by J. B. Trend
Jefferson and American Democracy, by Max Beloff
Pushkin and Russian Literature, by Janko Lavrin
Marx, Proudhon and European Socialism, by J. Hampden Jackson
Abraham Lincoln and the United States, by K. C. Wheare
Napoleon III and the Second Empire, by J. P. T. Bury
Alexander II and the Modernization of Russia, by W. E. Mosse
Gladstone and Liberalism, by J. L. Hammond and M. R. D. Foot
Livingstone and Africa, by Jack Simmons
Clemenceau and the Third Republic, by J. Hampden Jackson
Woodrow Wilson and American Liberalism, by E. M. Hugh-Jones
Lenin and the Russian Revolution, by Christopher Hill
Botha, Smuts and South Africa, by Basil Williams
Roosevelt and Modern America, by J. A. Woods

GLADSTONE

and

Liberalism

by

J. L. HAMMOND

and

M. R. D. FOOT

THE ENGLISH UNIVERSITIES PRESS LTD
102 Newgate Street
LONDON, E.C.1

FIRST PRINTED 1952
SECOND IMPRESSION 1962

PRINTED AND BOUND IN ENGLAND
FOR THE ENGLISH UNIVERSITIES PRESS LTD
BY HAZELL WATSON AND VINEY LTD, AYLESBURY

A General Introduction to the Series

THIS series has been undertaken in the conviction that there can be no subject of study more important than history. Great as have been the conquests of natural science in our time—such that many think of ours as a scientific age *par excellence*—it is even more urgent and necessary that advances should be made in the social sciences if we are to gain control of the forces of nature loosed upon us. The bed out of which all the social sciences spring is history; there they find, in greater or lesser degree, subject-matter and material, verification or contradiction.

There is no end to what we can learn from history, if only we will, for it is coterminous with life. Its special field is the life of man in society, and at every point we can learn vicariously from the experience of others before us in history.

To take one point only—the understanding of politics : how can we hope to understand the world of affairs around us if we do not know how it came to be what it is? How to understand Germany, or Soviet Russia, or the United States—or ourselves—without knowing something of their history?

There is no subject that is more useful or, indeed indispensable.

Some evidence of the growing awareness of this may be seen in the immense increase in the interest of the reading public in history and the much larger place the subject has come to take in education in our time.

This series has been planned to meet the needs and demands of a very wide public and of education—they are, indeed, the same. I am convinced that the most congenial, as well as the most concrete and practical, approach to history is the biographical, through the lives of the great men whose actions have been so much part of history, and whose careers in turn have been so moulded and formed by events.

The key-idea of this series, and what distinguishes it from any other that has appeared, is the intention by way of a biography of a great man to open up a significant historical theme; for example, Cromwell and the Puritan Revolution, or Lenin and the Russian Revolution.

My hope is, in the end, as the series fills out and completes itself, by a sufficient number of biographies to cover whole periods and subjects in that way. To give you the history of the United States, for example, or the British Empire or France, *via* a number of biographies of their leading historical figures.

That should be something new, as well as convenient and practical, in education.

I need hardly say that I am a strong believer in people with good academic standards writing once more for the general reading public, and of the public being given the best that the universities can provide. From this point of view this series is intended to bring the university into the homes of the people.

A. L. ROWSE.

ALL SOULS COLLEGE,
   OXFORD.

Contents

CHAPTER		PAGE
	A GENERAL INTRODUCTION TO THE SERIES .	V
I.	INTRODUCTION	I
II.	GLADSTONE'S FAMILY AND EDUCATION . (1809–33)	6
III.	THE FIRST INDUSTRIAL ENGLAND . .	27
IV.	GLADSTONE'S EARLY CONSERVATISM . (1833–46)	37
V.	A POLITICAL FREELANCE . . . . (1846–52)	53
VI.	THE CRIMEAN WAR PERIOD . . . (1852–9)	65
VII.	GLADSTONE AND PALMERSTON . . . (1859–67)	81
VIII.	GLADSTONE'S FIRST GOVERNMENT . . (1868–74)	106
IX.	BULGARIAN HORRORS . . . . (1875–9)	126
X.	IRELAND AGAIN . . . . . (1880–2)	135
XI.	REFORM AND EGYPT . . . . (1883–5)	150
XII.	HOME RULE . . . . . . (1885–6)	165
XIII.	THE LAST ACT . . . . . (1887–98)	186
XIV.	SUCCESSORS	201
	NOTE ON BOOKS	209
	TABLE OF DATES	211
	INDEX	215

NOTE

When Dr. Hammond died in 1949, he had only written part of this book; he had expressed the wish that I should finish it. Mrs. Hammond has most kindly read it all and given much helpful advice. My wife has also made many useful suggestions. I have been able to use some of Dr. Hammond's notes for chapters he had not begun to write, but of course take responsibility for the book in its final version.

M. R. D. F.

KEBLE COLLEGE,
OXFORD,
July 1951

Chapter One

Introduction

WHEN Gladstone died in 1898 it was universally recognised that he had been the leading figure of the nineteenth century in the history of Liberalism, not only in Great Britain but in Europe. 'No other statesman on our famous roll', said Morley, describing the tributes paid to his memory in different countries, 'has touched the imagination of so wide a world'; and it was the Liberal in him that was then most prominent and most praised. Yet for the first twenty-seven years of a career devoted to politics he had been a Conservative. He entered Parliament when he was twenty-three, and was a Minister in a Conservative Cabinet before he was thirty-four. When the Conservative party broke up in 1846 he remained loyal to its leader Sir Robert Peel, and was one of the most conspicuous of the band of 'Peelites' who wandered between the two great parties for the next thirteen years. With some of them he took part in the coalition under which we found ourselves at war in the Crimea. As late as 1858 it was generally expected that he would join Derby's Conservative Government formed that year, a government in which he was offered high office with prospects calculated to tempt ambition. When it fell in 1859, he gave a silent vote in its defence. In that year he first became a Liberal in any sense : he then decided that his agreement with Palmerston's Italian policy and the existing crisis in Italy made it his duty to join the Liberal Government which Palmerston was forming, and he remained in it until its Prime Minister died in 1865. From that time Gladstone was a Liberal leader, for by then he could be nothing less than a leader in any party to which he belonged. Yet it is clear that as a Peelite he looked back wistfully to his old party as a lost Eurydice. 'The key to my position', he said once, 'was that my opinions went one way, my lingering sympathies the other.'

Once a Liberal, Gladstone differed from all other Liberal leaders both in the tone of his politics and in the source of his principles. Yet his moral ascendancy over the party that he led was almost unrivalled. He was as much the idol of the working classes in the eighties as Palmerston had been, in the fifties, the idol of the England represented by the ten-pound householder. This is the more surprising because his chief competitor, Joseph Chamberlain, appealed directly to the interests and passions of the class that had now obtained the vote, whereas Gladstone was cold and sceptical about many projects that were close to their hearts. Cobden with his perfect mastery of the arts and methods of persuasion, and Bright with his Biblical eloquence and moving simplicity, never commanded so much support or such passionate loyalty.

Gladstone did not belong to the Manchester School; he had little liking for the Philosophic Radicals; he was not in touch with the group that worked for the emancipation of the Trade Unions in the sixties; he had nothing but hostility for the semi-republican movement led by Chamberlain and Dilke in the seventies; he mistrusted the enthusiasm for science that followed the great discoveries of Darwin. Though he became the leader of the party of reform, Balfour could write truthfully in 1895 that he 'is, and always was, in everything except essentials, a tremendous old Tory'. We get an idea of his isolation from the intellectual currents of his age in the last struggle of his life for Irish freedom from a letter by John Tyndall that appeared in *The Times* in 1887 : 'A former worshipper of the ex-Prime Minister said to me some time ago :—"Never in the history of England was there such a consensus of intellect arrayed against a statesman as that now arrayed against Mr. Gladstone. What a fall!" I rejoice to find this unanimity of judgment so specially illustrated among scientific men.' Thus of all public men of his time Gladstone occupied the most individual position, finding the origin and vitality of his ideas in sources strange if not alien to most Liberal minds, outside the contemporary influences that had produced Liberals of one kind or another, from Cobden to Chamberlain, from Huxley to Tyndall, from Bentham to Mill, and from Mill to Morley.

In this respect there is a similarity between his relation to Liberalism and that of his great opponent to Conservatism. Disraeli was the son of a man of letters who still belonged to the Jewish congregation when the future Prime Minister was born, and he had no hereditary ties with the mixed aristocracy of birth and wealth that formed the ruling class of the nineteenth century. Starting as a brilliant adventurer, he picked his way to the front in a world where he was despised for his birth and disliked for his race.

He was three parts a Chartist in the forties. Till the enfranchisement of the town labourer, he led the Conservative party on its own terms; that is, he gave his brains to its tactics. After 1867 he was in a strong enough position to put into effect some of the ideas he had preached in his revolutionary novel *Sybil* (published in 1845), but by that time his main interest was the expansion of British power in the world. About his career, externally a striking political success, he had at the last a sense of failure. When Hyndman, a young man, his head full of Marx and social revolution, went to visit him in his old age, he was warned against thinking he could make anything of the Conservative party. 'The moment you tried to realise it [collectivism] on our side you would find yourself surrounded by a phalanx of the great families who would thwart you at every turn : they and their women. . . . It is a very difficult country to move, Mr. Hyndman.' Gladstone was outwardly much less detached or excluded from the social forces of the age. His birth put him in the world of Peel; his marriage to a Glynne put him in the world of Palmerston; Eton and Oxford, where he was educated, were the nurseries of the governing class. But when we examine his intellectual development, we shall find that he was as lonely a figure as his great antagonist.

This isolation told against him. In 1858 the *Spectator* described him as the chief orator and the weakest man in the House of Commons, 'the most signal example, which the present time affords, of the man of speculation and scholarship misplaced and lost in the labyrinth of practical politics'. Yet it was also the cause of his strength. If he made so great an impression on the imagination of his age, it was because the political truths that guided him never came to him at second-hand, but were reached by the processes of a powerful and original mind. His association with Liberalism was inspiring and creative because his was the influence of a man ready for large ideas, steeped in history, and sustained by the study and understanding of the past. That was why he was able to give a character of his own devising to Liberalism and give strength to causes that had poor prospects when left to the play of the rivalries and stratagems of persons and parties.

Chapter Two

Gladstone's Family and Education
(1809–33)

GLADSTONE'S descent was Scottish on both
sides. His mother was a daughter of Andrew
Robertson, Provost of Dingwall in Ross-shire, of
Highland blood, and his father came of the Lowland
family of Gledstanes. With his attachment to Scott's
novels and his absorbing interest in primitive Greek
society, Gladstone took pleasure in the discovery that
the Gledstanes were Borderers. Finding that there was
a family of Gledstanes in Sweden, he hastened to the
conclusion that when the union of the crowns put an
end to border fighting, one branch had taken service
under Gustavus Adolphus and made its home in his
country. Gladstone's own family had come down in
the world, and then recovered its standing by success
in trade. His great-great-grandfather sold his ancestral
property at Arthurshiel in Lanarkshire, where his fore-
fathers had been lairds since 1551, and set up business
as a maltster at Biggar. His grandfather Thomas
moved to Leith, where he made his living as a corn-
dealer, and Gladstone's father John served in the
shop as a boy. Thomas Gladstone had enterprise and
ability, and his business expanded rapidly. He sent
ships to the Baltic. John Gladstone inherited his
qualities, and as a young man became a partner in
Messrs. Corrie, corn merchants in Liverpool. Later

6

he started business on his own account, and when the trade to the East was thrown open by the abolition of the monopoly of the East India Company, he sent to Calcutta the first ship that ever left Liverpool for that port.

It would have been fortunate for Gladstone as a politician if his father had confined his interest to India and the fortunes of his thriving East India house. But he looked West as well as East. This was natural enough for an energetic merchant in a port that had made its fortune out of the slave trade between Africa and the West Indies. By 1793 Liverpool had secured three-sevenths of the slave trade of Europe and grown from a hamlet to a prosperous city. During the last ten years of his career as a merchant, John Gladstone became the owner of large plantations of sugar and coffee in Jamaica and in British Guiana, with 1,609 slaves.

In 1823 there was a slave rising in Demerara, which was repressed with all the cruelty to be expected from panic-stricken men afraid for their lives as well as for their property. The agitation to which it led had a great influence in putting an end to slavery. An intrepid missionary named John Smith was tried by court-martial on charges of fostering discontent and encouraging the revolt. He was sentenced to death, and died in prison while the authorities were waiting for a decision from London on the court's recommendation to mercy. His death excited a horror that G. O. Trevelyan compared in its effect on public opinion at home to that of the execution of John Brown in 1859 on public opinion in the United States.

The Gladstone plantations were involved in these

7

bitter racial convulsions, and figured conspicuously in the debates on these events initiated by Brougham in 1824. Nor did the name of Gladstone relapse into an honourable obscurity when these storms had died down. John Gladstone, like his son, was fond of pen and ink, and he argued his case in frequent letters to the Press as well as in an open letter to Peel, published in 1830. This pamphlet impressed his opponents as an ingenious and telling apology, but he got into trouble with the House of Commons on the subject seven years later over an Order in Council permitting the West Indian planters to ship coolies from India on terms drawn up by the planters themselves. There were soon reports of ill-treatment of these coolies, both at sea and in the sugar-fields. A Commission sent to visit the Gladstone estates was able to give on the whole a favourable report, but the effect was to prolong the sinister reputation which John Gladstone's business zeal had given to a name that was to be associated with very different causes.

John Gladstone, besides being an active, perhaps in some connexions a too active, trader, was an active citizen. In 1811 he was given the freedom of Liverpool, and in 1818 he entered Parliament. He sat first for Lancaster and then for Woodstock; 'two boroughs', says Morley, 'of extremely easy political virtue'. He failed to secure a seat at Berwick in 1826. In 1837 he was defeated at Dundee by Sir Henry Parnell, afterwards Lord Congleton, whose more famous relative was to be closely involved in the fortunes of John Gladstone's famous son half a century later. Though out of Parliament, he was not inactive or lukewarm about public affairs. When the crisis over free trade came in 1846 he attacked Peel's 'stupendous experiment' in commercial policy,[1] and was much upset when his son supported the admission of Jews to Parliament in 1847. He died in 1851.

Gladstone's family circumstances affected his career in three ways.

He was brought up in an atmosphere of controversy over slavery in which political views were influenced by personal interest and family loyalty. Gladstone was not happy about slavery at the time; he urged his father to let him go to the West Indies and see for himself the condition of the family plantations. While John Gladstone was out of the House and had to confine himself to letters and pamphlets, the task of presenting and defending his ideas there fell to his sons. As late as 1840, the family was still defending its good name in this unhappy cause. In later life Gladstone reflected sadly on these early performances.

This was a passing influence. A lasting influence, on the other hand, was the personality of Canning, for Gladstone remained under that spell to the end of his life. John Gladstone was a great admirer of Canning, and it was through his influence that Canning was brought to Liverpool in 1812 to contest the seat. He defeated Brougham in a great contest, and sat for the city till 1822. John Gladstone often acted as his host, and Gladstone was taken down to the dining-room on one occasion (not long before his third birthday) to stand on a chair and say 'Ladies and Gentlemen'—his first recorded speech. 'I was

[1] Peel nevertheless made him a baronet. The baronetcy has now passed to one of the descendants of his son the Prime Minister; who more than once declined an earldom for himself.

9

bred', Gladstone told the House of Commons in 1866, 'under the shadow of the great name of Canning; every influence connected with that name governed the first political impressions of my childhood and my youth.' In one sphere this was a permanent influence, for in late life Gladstone liked to recall with pride and enthusiasm Canning's conduct as Foreign Minister. In early days the influence had not been altogether liberal, for it made Gladstone an anti-reformer and it encouraged his caution over the emanicpation of the West Indian slaves.

The son of a slave-owner and the youthful devotee of Canning, Gladstone was also a member of a family widely divided in opinion. At the time of his father's death, he wrote to a brother : 'Among few families of five persons will be found differences of character and opinion to the same aggregate amount as among us.' His father, as we have seen, was distressed by his views on Jewish disabilities; his brother Thomas differed from his politics, and his sister Helen's secession to the Church of Rome cost him more pain than any political disagreement. This early atmosphere, and the habits it encouraged of mind and speech, helped to develop some of Gladstone's most irritating qualities : his love of splitting hairs and his Protean dexterity and audacity in evading the confession of intellectual defeat. Hamilton said of him that he could distinguish between two propositions which the plain man would regard as identical.

At his greatest, Gladstone was the most striking figure of his century. He could make the meanest-minded man in the House of Commons think of himself for a brief hour as a member of an Olympian assembly and forget the base temptations of politics.

But when his self-will and his imperious nature mastered him, he was a different man; a man wasting and misusing his superb gifts on small victories. That was why Meredith said of him : 'Gladstone divides me. Half of him I respect deeply, and the other half seems not worthy of satire.'

Gladstone's scholastic bias, his intense interest in the Oxford Movement and in subtle distinctions in theology, helped to create this temperament; but it was partly due to this early atmosphere where fundamental family affection was combined with an incessant warfare of words.

William Ewart Gladstone was born in Liverpool on 29 December 1809. He was at Eton from September 1821 to Christmas 1827, and had the good fortune of a happy boyhood. In this he was luckier than Salisbury, who was so miserable that he was taken away for the sake of his health when he was fifteen. Gladstone always praised Eton as 'the queen of all schools', but Salisbury was haunted all his life by the memory of his perpetual persecution there, as Shaftesbury was haunted by the memory of his childhood terror of his parents. Salisbury was once asked how it was that he was so familiar with all the alleys and mews round his father's London house. He replied that when at Eton he was in such dread of meeting any of his school-fellows in the holidays that he avoided the larger streets when he went out alone. Gladstone entered on his school life under the wing of an elder brother, and this no doubt softened its rigours. He said once that Eton was a pleasant place if you liked boating and writing Latin verses; and he liked both. The rough manners of the place did not distress him as they had distressed Shelley fifteen years earlier. Later in life he said that if he had been given his choice, he would have lived in the Homeric age. He liked at Eton what he liked in the *Iliad* : he discovered that a good deal of primitive pugnacity was combined with the habit of discussion, a general feeling for fair play, and, above all, no great respect for wealth. 'No boy', he said, 'was ever estimated either more or less because he had much money to spend.'

And he made good friends at school. He shared everything, from his amusements on the river to his growing interest in literature, theology, and public affairs, with Arthur Hallam the subject of 'In Memoriam', of whose powers, so tragically extinguished in early life, his school friend thought to the end of his days no less highly than Tennyson.

Gladstone was happy, too, in attracting the notice of Edward Hawtrey, who had been one of the head boys of the school in Shelley's time, and was now an assistant master under the great flogger, Keate. Hawtrey afterwards became Head Master, and Gladstone said that Eton owed more to him than to any other of her sons during the century. It was Hawtrey who inspired Gladstone, three years after he had entered the school, with ambition and the belief that he had powers to develop. Till then Gladstone had remained 'stagnant without heart or hope', living not unhappily, playing cricket and football with moderate success, amusing himself in the evenings with chess and cards, enjoying most of all managing a small boat on the river. Under Hawtrey's inspiration, he moved into a more serious and a more spacious world. He became an active member of the Debating Society, where his maiden speech was a defence of the right of the poor to education, and joint editor of the *Eton Miscellany*, a review that had a short but vigorous life.[1]

Gladstone found that teaching at Eton was kept within narrow boundaries : 'When I was at Eton we knew very little indeed, but we knew it accurately.' Mathematics and science were held in poor respect, but religion did no better. 'The actual teaching of Christianity', Gladstone said later, 'was all but dead, though happily none of its forms had been surrendered.' But the account given in Gladstone's diary of the subjects he and his friends debated in their society and talked about, and of the books he read and discussed with Hallam, shows that, for boys who found their way into the higher reaches, Eton in his day was a first-rate preparation for public life. In his three unregenerate years he read Froissart, Hume, and Smollett, 'but only for the battles, and always skipping when I came to the sections headed "A Parliament"'. In the last three years he and his friends were discussing literature, history, and politics with the interest and ardour of well-read and cultivated men in contact with affairs. The sense of responsibility with which these boys

[1] He did not content himself with these opportunities for self-expression. His father, attacked in the columns of the *Liverpool Courier* for some inconsistencies in his economic arguments, was intrigued by the appearance in its pages of letters in his defence from a 'Friend to Fair Dealing'. It says much for the son's skill in concealing his style, or little for the father's skill in penetrating such a disguise, that John Gladstone never discovered the identity of his champion. The boy enjoyed listening to the family speculations on the subject. Perhaps this early success helped to delude him forty years later with the belief that when Prime Minister he could write an anonymous article on the Franco-Prussian War in the *Edinburgh Review* without risk of detection.

pursued truth and wisdom would have done credit to a Cabinet Minister. Gladstone and Hallam would have found themselves quite at home listening to the conversation at dinner at Holland House or at one of Samuel Rogers's breakfast parties. One of them, at any rate, would have been prepared at any moment to become something more than a listener.

Gladstone went up to Christ Church in October 1828, and at Oxford, as at Eton, he took things easily at first. Then he applied himself seriously to his studies, with such effect that he left Oxford, like Peel, with the prestige of a double First—in Greats and Mathematics. He tried for other distinctions, and in the competition for the Ireland scholarship, though unsuccessful, had the satisfaction of finding himself bracketed second with Robert Scott, of Liddell and Scott's *Lexicon*. The most interesting fact recorded of his performance is that his essay was marked 'desultory beyond belief'.[1] In later life his style varied from the terse and pointed writing to which is owed the high opinion Augustine Birrell formed of his literary skill to the involved and discursive treatment, pursuing every random turn that his fancy suggested, that filled other critics, like Disraeli, with contempt for the power and habits of his pen.

Gladstone's most intimate friend, Arthur Hallam, went to Trinity, Cambridge, and Gladstone thus had good means of comparing the education given at the two Universities. His verdict was strongly in favour of Oxford. At Cambridge pure scholarship was the chief interest in the pursuit of classical culture,

[1] An entry in Gladstone's diary during his final Schools remarked: 'On Friday we had in the morning historical questions. Wrote a vast quantity of matter, ill enough digested.'

whereas at Oxford the Greek and Latin masters were studied less for their form than for the philosophy they taught and for the history to which they gave a vivid life and a permanent significance. Certainly the Oxford treatment was the more congenial to Gladstone's tastes and more useful to his purposes in life.

Gladstone's Oxford life fell in a time of great political excitement. In 1829 Wellington's Government decided that it was less dangerous to concede than to continue to resist the Irish demand for Catholic Emancipation. This change of front was bitterly resented by many Tories, and nowhere was that resentment stronger than in Oxford. Peel, then Home Secretary, who represented the University in the House of Commons, resigned his seat on the question, and was defeated. Gladstone, as a loyal Canningite, was of course in favour of the new policy.

In the other great controversy of the time, that over Parliamentary Reform, he took a most active part. By this time he had won a great reputation at the Union, and a speech he made there against the Reform Bill, on 17 May 1831, had echoes outside Oxford. 'We all of us felt', said one of his contemporaries, 'that an epoch in our lives had occurred.' It was an important episode in Gladstone's life. A year later, the parliamentary borough of Newark fell vacant. The Duke of Newcastle was the patron of the borough, which survived the Reform Bill like many others under the domination of great magnates, and his son, Lord Lincoln, as friend and admirer of the young Gladstone, conveyed to the latter an invitation from the Duke, a diehard Tory, to contest the borough. Thus his undergraduate speech determined the time and circumstances of Gladstone's entry into the House of Commons.

During 1831, though his final examinations were approaching, Gladstone threw himself into the struggle against Reform with an ardour which suggested that he had no other care or purpose in life than the defeat of the bill that Burke and Canning had taught him to dread. He composed placards for the walls of Oxford, he drew up a pamphlet, he prepared a petition of portentous length, he rode his mare down the High in a lively anti-Reform demonstration, 'covered with mud from head to foot', and he went up to London in October to spend five nights listening to the debate in the Lords on the second reading of the bill. As he followed the arguments, the passions of the political partisan did not extinguish the independence of the literary critic, and he described the speech of Grey, the arch criminal in the proceeding, as 'most beautiful'. When the bill was rejected by 199 votes to 158, he wrote in his diary that : 'The consequences of the vote may be awful. . . . But it was an honourable and manly decision'.

From his struggle with the Reformers, he had now to turn to his struggle with the examiners. Of his strenuous effort in the last lap, which occupied him ten to twelve hours a day, he said that the bodily fatigue, the mental fatigue, and the anxiety as to the result made reading for a class a thing not to be undertaken more than once in a lifetime. When half a century later his superhuman power of concentration enabled him almost single-handed to put the gigantic Irish agrarian reform of 1881 on the Statute Book, he must have smiled at this solemn judgment.

His examiners, when he faced them in November, found that his efforts had not exhausted him, for he surprised them by wishing to continue discussion of a point of theology after they had tired of it. A month later he took the Mathematical School, an ordeal for which he calmed his nerves by taking sedatives on the doctor's prescription and absorbing long draughts of the meditative tranquillity of Wordsworth, a prescription of his own.

In December 1831 he left Oxford, with memories of the compliments paid to him by his examiners and of a series of triumphs at the Union, encouraged by the admiration of friends whom he respected, with every reason to expect that he would play a considerable part in the life of his country. But beneath this happy and confident surface there was another Gladstone, whose troubles and anxieties of spirit during his Oxford career need closer examination.

The fact about Gladstone that struck all who knew him was his immense energy, intellectual and physical. He walked great distances. He was constantly in the saddle. He entertained frequent parties and enjoyed incessant conversation. He was a voracious but not a desultory or superficial reader; he criticised; he learnt a great deal by heart, including most of Shelley; his pen was a Pegasus without a master. Two pages from his diary describing the end of the summer term of 1830 give a good impression of his vigour and his values :

'June 25. *Ethics*. Collections 9–3. Among other things wrote a long paper on religions of Egypt, Persia, Babylon; and on the Satirists. Finished packing books and clothes. Left Oxford between

17

5–6, and walked fifteen miles towards Leamington. Then obliged to put in, being caught by a thunderstorm. Comfortably off in a country inn at Steeple Aston. Read and spouted some *Prometheus Vinctus* there.

June 26. Started before 7. Walked eight miles to Banbury. Breakfast there, and walked on twenty-two to Leamington. Arrived at three, and changed. Gaskell came in the evening. *Life of Massinger.'*

All this vitality gave Gladstone great power of mind and body. But it was imprisoned power. He had been moulded in the strict Evangelical pattern by his mother, as Shaftesbury had been by his nurse. At Oxford he was still possessed by the inhibitions of this religion and disturbed by its panics. Fundamentally he was anxious and perplexed, unhappy except when he was absorbed in speech or action. Something of the self-tormenting analysis that makes Shaftesbury's diaries such a revelation of misery crept into Gladstone's introspecting mind. He had no reason to reproach himself with neglect of the active duties of his religion, for he was indefatigable then as later in church attendance. No undergraduate could have listened to more of the sermons of the day, and he listened with all his faculties and attention on the alert. He listened to Newman, then 'eyed with suspicion as a Low Churchman', to Whateley of whose anti-sabbatical doctrine he observed in his diary that it 'is, I fear, as mischievous as it is unsound'; to Keble for whom his admiration was tinged with anxieties ('Are all Mr. Keble's opinions those of scripture and the Church?'); to Blanco White, who spent his life drifting to and fro among different religions, who had returned for a time to the Established fold; and to a rogue preacher named Bulteel who, after causing a sensation by his strictures on the University in a sermon at St. Mary's, had been expelled from his pulpit for preaching in the open air. He enjoyed particularly a sermon in a Baptist chapel by the famous Presbyterian Dr. Chalmers, which lasted an hour and forty minutes. This robust endurance in the pew, which Gladstone owed to his Presbyterian blood, lasted through his life, and it enabled him to give just as close attention to a preacher without a glimmer of inspiration as he gave to such a master as Chalmers or Newman. Sometimes he wrote long critical letters to the preacher, and in one case, at any rate, he had the satisfaction of noticing an improvement in the doctrine taught in subsequent sermons.

Nor did he confine himself to hearing sermons. He taught in Sunday-school and he visited the sick and old. His diary for the Sunday before he faced the Mathematical Examiners is typical : 'Teaching in the school morning and evening. Saunders preached well on "Ye cannot serve God and Mammon". Read Bible and four of Horsley's sermons. Paid visits to old people.' Gladstone was at that time a strict Sabbatarian. Even later, when he begun to move away from the Evangelical orbit, he would not go to a dinner party at Peel's on a Sunday. He played cards, but not without occasional qualms, and when he heard of the time of Huskisson's death in 1830, struck down by one of Stephenson's engines at the opening of the Liverpool and Manchester Railway, he was shocked to remember that at the same moment he had been engaged in this frivolous amusement.

His Evangelical convictions made him look to the

Church as his proper sphere of duty, whereas his political interests drew him to public life. In 1830 the first influence was in the ascendant, and he wrote a very long letter to his father, who, he knew, would not like his decision and had urged him to choose the law for his profession. Explaining his point of view, he said that the attraction of religious orders had been gaining steadily upon him. 'Day after day it has grown upon and into my habit of feeling and desire. It has been gradually strengthened by those small accessions of power, each of which singly it would be utterly impossible to trace, but which collectively have not only produced a desire of a certain description, but have led me by reasonings often weighed and sifted and re-sifted to the best of my ability, to the deliberate conclusion which I have stated above. I do not indeed mean to say that there has been *no* time within this period at which I have felt a longing for other pursuits; but such feelings have been unstable and temporary; that which I now speak of is the permanent and habitual inclination of my mind.' He went on to speak of the moral wilderness of the world, which made him feel that he could not accept the pleasures of life or give his heart to its business 'while my fellow-creatures, to whom I am bound by every tie of human sympathies, of a common sinfulness and a common redemption, day after day are sinking into death'.

At this time in his life he was dominated by the belief that the world was drifting to eternal ruin from its pagan ignorance and habits. Newman put the same view in a terrible sentence in his *Apologia*: 'If I looked into a mirror and did not see my face, I should have the sort of feeling which actually comes upon me when I look into this living busy world and see no reflexion of its Creator.' Like Newman, Gladstone at first thought the place of a man who realised the condition of mankind was in the pulpit.

A letter he wrote to a brother at the same time discloses Gladstone's sense of the dangers of a political career for a man of his temperament, and makes it clear that the attractions of that career were stronger than he had allowed in his letter to his father. 'I am willing to persuade myself that in spite of other longings which I often feel, my heart is prepared to yield other hopes and other desires for this—of being permitted to be the humblest of those who may be commissioned to set before the eyes of man, still great even in his ruins, the magnificence and the glory of Christian truth. Especially as I feel that my temperament is so excitable that I should fear giving up my mind to other subjects which have ever proved sufficiently alluring to me, and which I fear would make my life a fever of unsatisfied longings and expectations.'

Gladstone's father wisely replied that it was too early to decide so grave a question, and that his immediate duty was to make what he could of himself in the Schools. Before Gladstone had to make up his mind, time and experience had taught him that the purpose he wished to serve might be served by other means. The character and the energy of the agitations and discussions of the time might well help to convince Burke's pupil that the most urgent need for his gifts was to be found in the field of public life. Religion and politics were much more closely associated than they had been in the eighteenth century.

This was natural, for the abuses choking public institutions, both at the centre and in local government, were nowhere more flagrant than in the Established Church. The Church had been regarded, like the pocket boroughs, as a great system of patronage and property. Bishoprics were plums for the members, relations, or dependants of the aristocracy. Parsons could hold several livings together, putting curates, miserably paid and insolently treated, to do their work in the parishes. A lively picture of the scandals of the time was given in Cobbett's *Legacy to Parsons,* published in 1835. In 1812, out of ten thousand incumbents five thousand were non-resident, and the revenues of 1,496 parishes were divided between 332 clergy. Even as late as 1838 there were over four thousand non-resident parsons. The removal of these abuses was one of the most remarkable of the successes of the Reformed Parliament. Both parties contributed to it. During the short life of the Government he formed in 1834, when William IV dismissed Melbourne, Peel set up the Ecclesiastical Commission, and Lord John Russell continued the good work Peel had started.

It is not surprising, then, that a serious and conscientious man with Gladstone's gifts who thought the first need of the world was the more effective teaching of Christian doctrine, should have looked to politics as the sphere in which he could give the most effective service to that cause. Gladstone entered politics, as he would have entered the pulpit, to serve the cause of Christian civilisation. The tale of his life shows how in his mind Christian civilisation came to embrace wider and wider horizons. Morley said that in respect of the fundamental dogmas of the Christian religion, Gladstone's opinions have no history. In one sense perhaps this is true, but it would be difficult to find a greater contrast than that between his later outlook on Christianity and the rigid and limited vision of his Oxford days.

The first stage in his expansion followed quickly on his leaving Oxford. He spent the spring and early summer of 1832 in Italy, and as he entered St. Peter's, the conception of the unity of Christianity in a visible Church, which was to occupy so much of his interest throughout his life, flooded his sensitive imagination. 'I had previously taken a great deal of teaching direct from the Bible, as best I could, but now the figure of the Church arose before me as a teacher too, and I gradually found in how incomplete and fragmentary a manner I had drawn divine truth from the secred volume.' He now began to move from his Oxford Evangelicalism to new and more spacious light; the process that, as we study his career, we find moulding his ideas of politics and religion throughout his life, keeping the two in close association.

In one of the innumerable papers that he wrote on religion in the course of his long life, he classified the three Christian schools to be found in England :

'(1) Those who accept the Papal monarchy : or the Ultramontane school.

(2) Those who, rejecting the Papal monarchy, believe in the visibility of the Church : or the Historical school.

(3) Those who, rejecting the Papal monarchy and the visibility of the Church, believe in the great central dogmas of the Christian system, the Trinity and the Incarnation . . . [or] the Protestant Evangelical school.'

What happened to Gladstone during the years following his departure from Oxford was that he passed from the third of these schools to the second. This can be seen as a stage in his progress towards Liberalism.

At first sight this is an astonishing fact. For the second school, famous in those years as the Oxford Tractarian Movement, had come to life in order to check the liberal teaching of the time. Newman drew up eighteen propositions of Liberalism which he condemned as false and irreligious. Liberalism seemed to him a great secularising force, seeking to discredit the belief that there was any positive truth in religion, and pressing for material reforms as sufficient in themselves to save mankind. So far was this hostility carried that even the scandals of the English and the Irish establishments were defended by these sublime votaries of the higher life, for such scandals when threatened by the secular arm symbolised the independence of the Church. When the Whigs proposed to reduce the Irish sees and to make a juster use of the surplus revenues of this privileged Church, the House of Lords, resisting in the name of the sanctity of property of every kind, found an ally in Newman, who described this reform as 'extinguishing half the candlesticks of the Irish Church'. How was it, then, that Gladstone, moving towards a school on guard for established interests, was also taking his first steps towards Liberalism?

The answer is that the Oxford Movement had two aspects. It was hostile to Bentham and his utilitarian philosophy, and in that sense it was hostile to the fundamental ideas that inspired a great many of the reforms of the nineteenth century. But it possessed a significance that made Mill, who, though a just and powerful critic of much of Bentham's teaching, was of

24

course one of the great Liberal forces of the age, give high praise to its services to culture. 'He used to tell us', said Morley, 'that the Oxford theologians had done for England something like what Guizot, Villemain, Michelet, Cousin had done a little earlier for France; they had opened, broadened, deepened the issues and meanings of European history; they had reminded us that history is European; that it is quite unintelligible if treated as merely local.'

Gladstone never became a Benthamite. To the end of his life, he would have found much to approve in Newman's criticisms of the men he condemned as putting too much emphasis on material civilisation. Some would say that this influence made him less responsive than he should have been to such causes as those of municipal improvement and social development; that because he felt as strongly as Newman 'that good and evil were not lights and shadows passing over the surface of society but living powers springing from the depths of the human heart', he underestimated the influence of material surroundings on character and happiness. But the other influence of the Oxford Movement was far more important in his life, in drawing him towards the purposes that were to give him his special place in history. For this change took him away from the insularity of the Evangelical School; insularity in culture and in sympathy. 'The Evangelical Movement', he said later, 'with all its virtues and merits, had the vice of individualising religion in a degree perhaps unexampled'; on another occasion he pointed out that 'it had a code with respect to amusements, which was at once rigid and superficial . . . it did not ally itself with literature, art, and general cultivation'. He thought that it was because Evangelicalism was 'eminently narrow and inconsequent as a system' that some of the most famous of those who passed like him from the third to the second of the schools he defined, found their way afterwards into the first, cherishing the comforts it offered to minds in search of a large historical discipline and unity in which to anchor their faith. In speaking of the bias against liberty that the prevalent atmosphere of Oxford teaching in his day created in his mind, he observed that a similar bias was to be found in his Evangelical atmosphere. Thus it was that in moving into the orbit of a school that was the most famous of the opponents of Liberalism, he found an inspiration that helped to make him half a century later the greatest Liberal in Europe.[1]

[1] Shaftesbury (born in 1801) was the only one of the four leading men, born in the first decade of the century and brought up in Evangelical homes, who held to that creed all through his life. Newman, his exact contemporary, became a Roman Catholic in 1845; Manning, seven years younger, in 1851. Gladstone, whose own eventual religious position was anchored on the Anglo-Catholic shore of the gulf between the Anglican and Roman Churches, said in 1879 that 'Oxford was only the posting-house, where the most eminent and powerful of the seceders slept on their journey towards Rome'.

Chapter Three

The First Industrial England

INTO what sort of society did Gladstone bring the beliefs, the temperament, the outlook described in the last chapter?

The French Revolution, which began twenty years before he was born, preoccupied the political mind of the early nineteenth century much as the Russian Revolution preoccupies that of the twentieth. Opinion in England was divided on the question then as now: almost universal patriotism at moments of national danger; at other times widespread sympathy with the revolutionaries, especially among the poor. But the English poor of 1830 were very different from the poor of 1930: often illiterate, much less well clothed and well fed, few of them (outside London) were not countrymen themselves or the sons of countrymen. While the French had been preaching in the seventeen-nineties the brotherhood of man, the English had been practising a revolution of their own, an economic and not a political revolution, that seemed to be founded on the negation of brotherhood as it developed the relations between master and man.

New wealth was generated in England, at the end of the eighteenth century and early in the nineteenth, by the application of recent scientific discoveries to everyday life. Factories, towns, and population all greatly expanded. This wealth enabled England

27

to save Europe from the great Napoleon, but it was not directly employed to satisfy the needs of the English people. A false confidence, inspired by the mechanical triumphs of the Industrial Revolution, misled many of the thinkers of the age, and they believed that the enterprise and initiative of the private individual, directed towards economic gains, would automatically bring prosperity for everyone.

It turned out that prosperity could not come simply through unaided private expansion, numerous as were the inventions and countless the opportunities which that expansion exploited. Wealth was vastly increased, but suffering increased with it; to limit the suffering, especially in the new forms brought on by new processes in industry, as well as to foster trade, some State action was needed. But it was not possible for individual manufacturers or individual statesmen to see the country's economic life as a whole in an age when economic and statistical analysis had hardly begun to develop. Moreover, many of the country's institutions were suffering from the indolent self-satisfaction that had in too many spheres followed the English revolution of the seventeenth century, and were in need of an overhaul. Parliament itself, though vigorous enough, was based on an erratic franchise system, against which a reasonable case that it was unrepresentative could easily be made out. Macaulay pointed to a remarkable contrast between the vitality of the British people in the eighteenth and early nineteenth centuries and their inefficient and decrepit institutions.

Some attempts at improvement were made in the seventeen-eighties by Burke and by the young Pitt, but both were distracted from their reforming intentions by the danger, and then the fact, of war with France. During the long war, which lasted from 1793 to 1815 with only two brief intermissions, strategy seemed more important than politics, and any move towards a more democratic franchise could too easily be denounced as a treacherous step along the path that had led Paris to the Terror. During the war the development of industry was not altogether held up, and in some trades (cotton and iron particularly) managed to make much progress. The old ruling class, of English and Scottish landowners and their friends, was strengthened by the addition of merchants and bankers, and even a few manufacturers, such as Peel's father.

Yet in the years after Waterloo the rising middle class of manufacturers and traders, the class that Disraeli so much disliked and despised, sought to secure a larger share in the control of the government machine. Cautious attempts were already being made to begin again the process of refurbishing and modernising it that had been arrested by the war; Peel as Home Secretary and Huskisson at the Board of Trade effected some law and tariff reform, and just after Canning's death in 1827 the threat of civil war in Ireland persuaded the Tories to relax the old restrictions on Irish Roman Catholics. Civil war was threatened nearer home by the partly organised English town workers, anxious to play a part of their own in politics, who made parliamentary reform their cause. This part was denied them when, during the three tumultuous years 1830, 1831, 1832, a measure of reform acceptable both to the upper and the middle classes was hammered out. The great Reform Bill, passed in 1832, established a middle-class electorate, but the workers were satisfied for the time being and the threatened revolution was averted.

But parliamentary reform was not the only kind of reform that was possible or that feeling at the time desired. The great Reform Bill marked both the climax of the reforming work of the old system and the beginning of new work on more extensive lines. As Gladstone remarked forty-five years later, there was an active desire in the country for reform of all sorts for a generation after 1832, and it was not until the outbreak of the Crimean War in 1854 that the reforming movement was arrested. During this generation some real progress was made in laying the foundations of a more efficient society. The Whig Governments of Grey and Melbourne (1830–41) were led by Ministers who did not expect a great deal from politics, and Melbourne became a byword for sloth; but under them, under Peel (1841–6), and under Russell (1846–52), inquiries were conducted and measures passed which affected almost the whole field of public life.

The new laws were none of them considered from the point of view of poor men. They were prepared, to appeal to the new electorate, by men of property, whether of the old or of the new ruling class (the two classes mixed easily, as we have seen in Gladstone's case, at the public schools and at the universities). The struggle of the poor for better conditions, marked already by the fatal clashes between crowds and troops at Peterloo and Bonnymuir in 1819 and 1820, included the revolt in south-eastern England in the winter of 1830–1 when, like the Luddites of twenty years before, starving labourers broke up the machines that seemed to be turning them out of work. The struggle continued, with the transportation of the Dorset labourers in 1834 and the Newport rising of 1839. The organization of the Chartist Movement alarmed the governing classes; in 1848 Gladstone (like Louis Napoleon) found himself among the special constables enrolled to protect London against the threatened Chartist march that turned out a fiasco.

Yet with the change of Government from Tory to Whig in 1830, a more energetic era in British administration had begun and more serious efforts were made by successive Cabinets to overtake the neglect of generations. The new Poor Law—criticised by a few such independent men as Walter of *The Times,* the young Disraeli, and Cobbett—set up a harsh and inhuman system whose rigours led to acute discontent. In some parts of England hostility was so widespread that the severer clauses were never put into effect. Yet it was passed in 1834 with the utmost confidence, and was no less rational than it turned out to be cruel. The Municipal Corporations Act of 1835 was in some respects a disappointing measure, but it substituted organised government in the towns for the anomalies of a system under which the towns had fallen into the hands of small and generally corrupt oligarchies, and the most elementary social services had been neglected. Popular education received a (tiny) national grant for the first time in 1833, the Central Criminal Court was established in 1834, inspection of schools began in 1839. The Factory Act of 1833, though it left children over thirteen unprotected, created a factory inspectorate, and thus introduced a principle that was to have a most beneficent influence. Inquiries into health in towns produced results in time, but more slowly; for though the Whigs introduced two unsuccessful bills in 1841, one forbidding the building of back-to-back houses, the first Public Health Act was not passed until 1848. (Back-to-back houses were not finally forbidden until 1909.) Fourteen years of agitation by Lord Ashley led to the eventual triumph of the Ten Hours' Bill, which limited the hours of work of women and children (and consequently of men) to ten hours a day in textile factories. It was passed in 1847.

These measures were only some of the more important in a series of reforms. Four influences may be picked out as having specially contributed to the possibility of any reform : first and most important, the philosophy of Jeremy Bentham (1748–1832) and his disciples, of which a criticism must be reserved to the next chapter in connexion with some work of Gladstone's own. Men wanting some guiding light in an atmosphere of confusion and despondency found it in his teaching; Chadwick, the greatest administrative force of the age, had been his private secretary. The attack on the stagnant disorder of politics, and, above all, on the power of superstition to arrest reform during the dark hours of the French wars and the panics that succeeded them, was led and guided by his vigour and his lucid genius. Meredith's tribute to revolutionary France as the nation that first shook the dead from living men could be applied to Bentham's services to his own country.

A second influence was that of the humanitarians, who provided the political aspect of the Evangelical Movement in the Church. Wilberforce, the contemporary and friend of Pitt, had led them to their first triumph in 1807, when the slave trade was abolished; he died in 1833, a few weeks before the final abolition of slavery itself within the British Empire. Thereafter their greatest leader was Ashley (who became Lord Shaftesbury in 1851), whose overpowering interest in the relief of human misery led him into many social crusades. To these he sacrificed his political ambition, but earned instead of high office a fame that has outlived that of almost all his contemporaries.

Thirdly, the nineteenth century had inherited from the eighteenth, together with a mass of problems, a custom that was of great potential value. Parliament had been regarded less as a legislative body than as the custodian of the rights of the citizen against the executive power. In practice this custom could be more of a protection for persons of the governing class than for others; over enclosures, for instance, private bill committees helped the powerful much more than the rank and file (who had still available for their defence the valuable traditions of the English common law). But it had led to the habit of setting up committees of inquiry into alleged grievances. This habit acquired added importance under the reformed House of Commons; and in retrospect even Marx, horrified though he was at the condition of the workers of London, where he lived in exile after 1849, recognised that the extensive social inquests carried out by parliamentary committees were of much value for the student and thus for the reformer.

The fourth significant factor in British public life at this time was the character of its Conservative party, which differed from the Conservative parties of the rest of Europe in that it was not merely a party for holding fast, or frankly a party of reaction. Under the different influences of Canning and of Peel, the Conservative party had also become a party of reform. Gladstone, looking back in extreme old age, thought that an important stage in this process had been the discovery that the first great step in 1832 down the slope of reform had not taken the country over the brink of the abyss of revolution. It is certainly true that after 1832 the extreme Tories dropped out of Conservative politics, and Peel created a Conservative party in which the country landowners, the party's permanent backbone, were wise enough and bold enough not to sulk after defeat like the French upper classes, but to accept the necessity of some reform. Hence when the Whigs fell in 1841 they were succeeded, not by a Government anxious to preserve things as they were, but by one ready to remove abuses that seemed to stand in the way of British prosperity.

Peel's Government of 1841-6, as we shall see, effected vital changes in the British economy, modernising the structure of finance and trade, and laying foundations for the great expansion of British commerce in the second half of the century. Peel even dared to reimpose (at sevenpence in the pound) the income tax which Pitt had introduced in 1798 to meet the demands of the war with revolutionary France. It had been discarded in 1816 after a demonstration of schoolboy spirits in the House of Commons. That it needed no ordinary courage to reimpose this hated tax is shown by Cobden's prophecy that Peel's income tax would 'do more than the Corn Law to destroy the Tories.'

But the effect of these reforms was not immediate.

34

The forties were years of active and widespread discontent, which has perplexed many economists, who point out that the purchasing power of wages had for the most part gone up, and that in this respect the British poor were almost the best off in Europe. This discontent was partly due to the deplorably bad conditions in the crowded new towns and partly to a feeling among working men that they were shut off from opportunities and from political power. In ancient Greece, rich men spent their money on beautifying their city and continued to live plainly; little communal enjoyment was provided by the typical successful manufacturer of the English Industrial Revolution, who spent his money within his lavish household and his firm. The Ten Hours' Act, the first recognition of the right of the working classes to leisure, began the work of emancipating them from Graham's terrible formula that the lot of the labourer was eating, drinking, working, and dying, and began the work of civilising the new forces of raw wealth. The Public Health Act of 1848 was followed gradually by the introduction of such amenities as parks and libraries, that helped to diffuse self-respect. In the longer run, the prosperity that followed the great economic reforms of Peel's Government, though it was most unequally shared, affected the general conditions of social life, and made some slow progress possible. Thus after the middle of the century life became a little less bleak and bitter. The first harsh encounter with the savage logic of the Industrial Revolution was succeeded by adaptation, the great principle of British history, applied through the unique institution of the British Parliament. It was through Parliament that Gladstone, like almost every other famous statesman in British history since Elizabeth's reign, rose to prominence and power. We must trace now the course that he took in the sphere of life that he had chosen for himself, and the reasons that led him to leave the party in whose ranks his political career began.

Chapter Four

Gladstone's Early Conservatism
(1833–46)

GLADSTONE entered the House of Commons in January 1833, after an election in which he had given something of a shock to his patron, the Duke of Newcastle, by a sentence in his address deploring the 'inadequate remuneration of labour'. Apart from this reference, social questions were not prominent in the address. His main preoccupations were revealed in the sections of it referring to religion. He stood for the union of Church and State; the maintenance in particular of the Irish establishment; a system of Christian education for the West Indian slaves, and no emancipation till such education had fitted them for it.[1]

Gladstone made his mark at once as a debater. His first success was gained in the defence of his family name in the unhappy cause with which John Gladstone had associated it. In the course of the debate on the bill for the gradual abolition of slavery in the colonies, brought in and passed by the Whig Government in 1833, Howick, son of Grey the Prime Minis-

[1] It is interesting to note that Burke, who was Gladstone's teacher alike in his Conservative and Liberal career, had inserted in the sketch of a Negro Code which he sent to Dundas in 1792 a provision that any Negro who sought legal freedom was to supply 'a certificate from the Minister of his district . . . of his regularity in the duties of religion'.

ter, made an attack on the manager of the Gladstone estates in Demerara, calling him a 'murderer of slaves'. Gladstone replied to this speech a few days later. He met Howick's charges, but admitted that cruelty was inevitable under slavery. For that reason he held that the British people should set itself in good earnest to slavery's extinction, though he deprecated emancipation before the slaves had been prepared for it. The speech was admired by men of all parties. Althorp, leader of the House, praised it to the King in private; and in debate Stanley the Colonial Secretary, who was in charge of the bill, paid it high compliments. 'He had never listened with greater pleasure to any speech'; the Member for Newark had argued his case 'with a calmness, a clearness, and a precision, which might operate as an example to older Members'. Gladstone was afterwards ashamed of this success, but he was not more cautious about emancipation than his leader Peel, or as hostile as his future rival Disraeli. In 1851 Disraeli strongly condemned the anti-slavery movement : 'The history of the abolition of slavery by the English and its consequences, would be a narrative of ignorance, injustice, blundering, waste, and havoc, not easily paralleled in the history of mankind.'

Gladstone was respected from the first for his gifts, but he was then out of sympathy with the active currents of popular feeling. He was a good deal shut up in his religious interests and out of tune with the House of Commons. For public life when he entered it was animated, as we have seen, by the spirit of Bentham and the passion for improvement. All sorts of movements were sharing this inspiration and guiding the vitality of the age into the service of one cause

or another. Prominent among them was the Society
for the Diffusion of Useful Knowledge, of which Pea-
cock made fun in *Crotchet Castle* where he nicknamed it 'The Steam Intellect Society'. Newman described these enthusiasts as believing that the printing
press could do with mind what the steam engine had
done with matter. There was much shallow philosophy and crude optimism behind these various projects for overtaking the gross ignorance of the time
and developing popular culture. But England owed
a great debt to the impulse, deriving from Bentham,
for tidying public life, for shaking the omnipotence
of habit, and for spreading knowledge and intelli-
gence. Acton, speaking of the intuition that started
Bentham on his mission of disentangling the innumerable injustices of the law, said that 'the day when that
gleam lighted up the clear and hard mind of Jeremy
Bentham is memorable in the political calendar beyond the entire administration of many statesmen'.
Mill, a critic as well as a follower, praised him as
the Hercules who cleared away the superstitions that
protected abuses in law and administration. Bentham
started on his crusade as a young man and grew old
in its service before he found much support. His clear
mind, with its vigour and daring, asking of every institution what purpose it served, substituting science
for custom as a guide in politics, gave him such intellectual leadership that hardly any public man of note
escaped his influence. The course of the French Revolution had turned many who had started with great
enthusiasm for natural rights into hardened conservatives. Bentham substituted a new gospel for that of
natural rights, the 'Principle of Utility' which advo-
cated 'the greatest happiness of the greatest number',

39

and his incisive and brilliant imagination when it turned this searchlight on to British public institutions was able to discover great scope for action.

Gladstone, who in his old age was regarded as a reckless man with revolutionary ambitions, started life not as a reformer eager for a share in such bold enterprises but as a Conservative on guard for principles that seemed to him in great danger. In particular he mistrusted the dominant influence among active reformers. In January 1832 he wrote a long letter to his father on the subject of utilitarian philosophy. This, like many of his letters, runs to several pages, but is summarised by Morley in these few sentences : 'New principles, he says, prevail in morals, politics, education. Enlightened self-interest is made the substitute for the old bonds of unreasoned attachment, and under the plausible maxim that knowledge is power, one kind of ignorance is made to take the place of another kind. Christianity teaches that the head is to be exalted through the heart, but Benthamism maintains that the heart is to be amended through the head.' [1] Gladstone saw in this doctrine that enlightened self-interest was the true guide to conduct, private and public, a danger such as Ruskin saw in the onrush of industrialism. To Ruskin the machine age, devouring the beauty of nature and of noble and ancient buildings that repeopled the silent past, threatened to impoverish the imagination and the

[1] In truth 'spiritual animal' wer a term for man
nearer than 'rational' to define his genus;
Faith being the humanizer of his brutal passions,
the clarifier of folly and medicine of care,
the clue of reality, and the driving motiv
of thatt self-knowledge which teacheth the ethick of life.
BRIDGES, *Testament of Beauty*, IV, 1131.

memories of the British people. To Gladstone Benthamism stood for something like the machine age in the world of consciousness. Its analysis of motive and its simplification of relationships of life seemed to him to impoverish men's spiritual faculties and to destroy the sense of obligation and the Christian spirit of fellowship in which he found the ties that unite men and keep societies together.

To appreciate Gladstone's view, it is useful to turn to Mill's criticism of Bentham. The hardness of Bentham's mind of which Acton spoke was accompanied by a certain hardness of character, of which the limitations were well set out by Mill in 1838. Mill objected that Bentham described a world that was a collection of persons each pursuing his separate pleasure or interest, in which the law, religion, and public opinion, imposing their several sanctions, served to prevent more jostling than was unavoidable. Mill thought that Bentham's view of human nature was narrow and superficial from lack of the imagination that enables one man to enter into the minds of other persons and other ages. 'Self-consciousness, that dæmon of the men of genius of our time, from Wordsworth to Byron, from Goethe to Chateaubriand, and to which this age owes so much both of its cheerful and its mournful wisdom, never was awakened in him. How much of human nature slumbered in him he knew not, neither can we know. He had never been made alive to the unseen influences which were acting on himself, nor consequently on his fellow-creatures. Other ages and other nations were a blank to him for purposes of instruction. He measured them but by one standard; their knowledge of facts, and their capability to take correct views of utility and merge all

41

other objects in it.' In another passage Mill described Bentham as a half-thinker, though this was less disparaging than it sounds, for he added that 'Almost all rich veins of original and striking speculation have been opened by systematic half-thinkers'. But a half-thinker, however important his discoveries, is a man who misses equally important truth.

The truth that Bentham missed was to be found in the pages of Coleridge's study of Church and State. Where Bentham applied to institutions and customs the cold analysis of rationalism, Coleridge applied the sympathetic vision of historical imagination. Gladstone, so far as he was a follower of any contemporary thinker, was a follower of Coleridge. But Gladstone was better able at this stage in his career to discern the danger in Benthamism than to provide against it. Just as the rationalist spirit when carried to excess makes a man a vandal, so the historical spirit carried to excess makes a man a champion of abuses. Gladstone in the first flush of his missionary zeal was as crude in his plans for defending the spiritual interests of the nation as the men whose cocksure remedies for ignorance and misgovernment Newman had derided. For he resisted all proposals for reforming the Church of England, and thought that to defend it as it stood was the true way of defending the spiritual interests that were threatened by a secularising flood. Not content with action in Parliament, he devoted himself to preparing a long book on *The State in its Relations with the Church,* published in 1838. Lathbury observed that the book expressed a theory of the subject that Gladstone was outgrowing as he wrote it; that he began it as an Evangelical and finished it as a High Churchman. Its ultimate conclusion was startling : it was that the State has a conscience that is capable of distinguishing between truth and error, and that it is its duty to give official support to the true religion and no other. He pushed this doctrine so far as to defend the maintenance of the Irish Church with all its wealth and privileges, from the belief that it might convince the most Catholic people in the world of the truth of the Protestant religion.

A phrase in Macaulay's article on this book in the *Edinburgh Review* describing Gladstone as the rising hope of stern and unbending Tories has passed into history, but it is true, as Lathbury says, that the most important criticism of the book came from John Keble, who observed : 'however fearful the view which may be taken of a world antichristianized by the downfall of Establishments, might not a sadder picture be drawn, and one at least as likely to be realized, of a Church turned antichristian by corrupt Establishments?' Gladstone himself accepted this criticism, which shows that his mind was moving away from his main thesis as soon as it was stated.

The book made a remarkable stir. It was not surprising that the bishops of the establishment should welcome it, but it was treated with sympathy and respect by men as various as Wordsworth, Arnold, and the Prussian diplomat and theologian Bunsen, who said that Gladstone was 'the first man in England as to intellectual power' and had 'heard higher tones than any one else in this land'. Even Irish Catholic bishops forgave the book its Protestant heresies in their sympathy with its spirit. One man, and that a person of great importance to Gladstone, took a very different view. Peel, who detested the Oxford Movement, was gravely disturbed. 'That young man', he said, 'will ruin his fine political career if he persists in writing trash like this.'

When Peel spoke of the 'fine political career' that Gladstone was in danger of ruining by theological excitement, he was in a good position for judging his capacity and prospects. For he had been so much impressed by Gladstone's early speeches that he had taken him into the Government that he formed in 1834. Late in that year William IV dismissed Melbourne, who had succeeded Grey as Prime Minister, alleging that his Government had been too much weakened by the loss of Althorp (who had to leave the Commons for the Lords) to go on with credit or self-confidence. Peel made Gladstone first a Lord of the Treasury and then Under-Secretary for the Colonies. Peel's Government lasted only a few months, for the general election early in 1835, though it increased the Conservatives' strength by about a hundred, still left their opponents with a large majority. But those months taught Gladstone a great deal, for they introduced him to the work and discipline of administration, as well as to colonial problems, and both experiences helped to liberalise his mind. Peel thus knew something of his quality, both as a debater and as a junior Minister.

In the years of opposition following Peel's resignation in April 1835, Gladstone was in close touch with the Conservative leaders, for he was invited to attend meetings of what we should call the Shadow Cabinet when colonial questions were under discussion. These questions were among the chief anxieties of the time. When the general election of 1841 brought Peel to power with a large majority (some 367 to 286), he hoped to find himself in the Cabinet. He was therefore mortified when he was offered the post of Vice-President of the Board of Trade. He was ignorant and indifferent about the subjects handled in the department. Peel suspected that any son of so astute a merchant as John Gladstone would take quickly to these affairs, and wished to give this young mystic, his head lost in the confusing clouds of theology, some practical difficulties to resolve, difficulties demanding discipline and concentration in place of subtleties and metaphysics. Gladstone would have liked Ireland, but Peel knew that Gladstone's religion would not mix happily with Ulster's or with Dublin's.

The young Minister confessed his disappointment in his diary, where he wrote that he thought of politics as the science of governing men, and he had been given the task of governing packages. But he was soon immersed in the cares and problems of his office, and quickly justified Peel's intuition; for instead of finding his work as distasteful as he had expected, he found it fascinating. As his chief, Lord Ripon, was in the House of Lords and from the point of view of this work a nonentity, Gladstone was in a position of importance. He showed his sense of personal responsibility and his capacity for constructive suggestion by proposing to Peel that the latter should impose a progressive house tax instead of reimposing the income-tax. Peel rejected the suggestion, but not without giving it flattering consideration and consulting Graham and Stanley, who agreed with him.

On the Corn Laws, Gladstone prepared a long paper, at Peel's request, and the study of the problem which this task demanded brought him to the conclusion that Peel might go farther in reducing duties in 1842 than he proposed. He argued his case in a long discussion with the chief Ministers, and in a private interview with Peel he hinted at retirement when his views were rejected. Peel was 'thunderstruck' by this display of self-will, and he went so far as to say that Gladstone's resignation on this question would 'endanger the existence of the administration'. Fortunately Gladstone's immense energy was soon absorbed in the vast process of revising the tariff. Duties were taken off, or reduced on, no fewer than 750 articles, and Gladstone made 129 speeches in the Commons in the course of the relevant debates. An impression of one difference between that House of Commons and the modern one is given by a sharp controversy on the subject of fish. Although duties had been scattered with a lavish hand on every kind of food, two fish had escaped : turbot and lobster. Peel proposed to put these luxury fish on the same footing as the fish eaten by the poor, but this was too much for the rich men in Parliament and his Government had to give way.

Many years later Gladstone said that of the four great revisions of the tariff with which he had been concerned, those of 1842, 1845, 1853, and 1860, the first cost six times as much trouble as the other three put together. Gladstone had hardly given a thought to trade or finance before he entered this Government, but he quickly made himself such a master of their complex problems that Peel declared that a more admirable combination of ability, extensive knowledge, temper, and discretion had never been exhibited in the annals of Parliament. This was high praise from a chief who had to suffer more than once from his junior colleague's persistence in pressing points of view on which he disagreed with his leader.

In 1843 Ripon was transferred to the Indian Board of Control, and Peel offered Ripon's place to Gladstone. After some characteristic and tiresome hesitation, Gladstone accepted. He feared that in becoming a member of the Cabinet he would accept responsibility for practices and measures which he disapproved : notably the growing of opium in India and the proposed union of two Welsh bishoprics. Manning, schooled like Gladstone in casuistry, helped him to resolve the second difficulty. Peel treated his scruples with patience, and Gladstone took the opportunity of apologising for his threat to resign in 1842 over the corn duties. So, at the age of 33, Gladstone entered the Cabinet after ten years in Parliament.

Gladstone had thus a principal share in the fiscal revolution that was necessary to the prosperity of British trade. He had also a large part in bringing about the changes in company law, to which Professor Cole attributes some of the better temper of the later years of the Industrial Revolution. His effort to check the wild speculation in railway shares and the mushroom growth of railway companies by the Joint Stock Companies Regulation Act of 1844 led to the adoption of the limited liability principle. In his Railway Act of 1844 he gave the State full rights of intervention in the concerns of railway companies and the option to purchase lines at the end of a certain term.[1] He gave

[1] Gladstone, when Chancellor of the Exchequer in 1864, outlined a plan for the State purchase of railways, the lines to be leased to commercial firms and controlled by a Government Board, but Palmerston dismissed it as 'a wild and more than doubtful Project'.

poorer travellers a great boon : hitherto on some lines third-class carriages had had neither seats nor roofs. Gladstone's Act created the Victorian parliamentary train to be composed of carriages protected from the weather with a maximum charge of a penny a mile. Fierce opposition from railway interests succeeded in drawing the teeth of other parts of his measure, but its provisions showed that Gladstone was not afraid of taking power for the State and that he was concerned to relieve the hardships of the poor.

In the same spirit he intervened to deliver a class of ill-used men from a serious grievance. These were the 'coal whippers' in the London docks, men who carried coal in baskets from the ships to barges or the wharf. These men were engaged and discharged at public-houses, and a man could only get and keep employment by a publican's good-will. That good-will depended on expenditure in the public-house of a good part of the scanty wages earned, varying from 13s. 3d. to 19s. 6d. a week. Gladstone brought in and passed a bill eliminating the public-houses and setting up a central office in their place; this reform won him the lasting gratitude of the coal whippers.

In 1845 Gladstone brought this useful and promising career at the Board of Trade to an abrupt conclusion by a decision that helps to explain what his friend Henry Taylor, a shrewd observer of public affairs, meant when he said that a statesman needs a strong rather than a tender conscience. Peel, who was anxious to pursue a conciliatory policy in Ireland, resolved to increase the grant to the Roman Catholic college of Maynooth and put it on a permanent basis. Gladstone thought this right and wise. But he felt that it would be improper for him to remain in the

Cabinet, because this policy would be contrary to the views he had set out in his book on Church and State seven years earlier. His scruples mystified everyone, and his long explanation in the House of Commons did nothing to dissipate confusion. 'What a marvellous talent is this!' said Cobden. 'Here have I been listening with pleasure for an hour to his explanation, and I know no more why he left the Government than before he commenced.' Greville thought the explanation ludicrous: 'Everybody said that he had only succeeded in showing that his resignation was quite uncalled for.'

Gladstone was thus out of the Cabinet during some of the most important discussions and decisions of the century, for in the autumn of that year came the crisis which broke up the Conservative party. The catastrophe of the Irish potato famine, followed by a wet autumn in England, had put a terrible force behind the agitation for Corn Law Repeal, and Peel told his Cabinet in December that he had decided for the gradual abolition of the Corn Laws. Stanley, a very important member of the Cabinet, dissented, and Peel resigned. Lord John Russell, given to impulsive action without consultation with his colleagues, had published a letter in favour of total and immediate repeal, for he had been quick to grasp the change in the situation produced by these natural calamities. He failed to replace Peel, nominally because of difficulties within his party, but really, as was suspected, because he did not relish a struggle with the Lords in which he might expect to be defeated. Peel, he saw, would be in a stronger position for overcoming the hostility of the peers. Peel then set about reconstructing his Government as a Repeal Government. Wellington, though he complained that 'rotten potatoes have put Peel in his damned fright', consented to take office, and, thanks to his immense personal authority, Corn Law Repeal was carried not only in the Commons but in the Lords. There the majority was 47; 93 peers recorded their protests in the Journals of their House.

Peel, though successful in carrying this measure, suffered acutely at the hands of Disraeli, who led a party revolt. Gladstone said afterwards that Peel was overwhelmed by Disraeli's attacks and that he was helpless in the hands of his tormentor. Gladstone never forgave Disraeli his bitter invective against Peel, just as the Queen never forgave Gladstone his bitter invective against Disraeli thirty years later. Perhaps if he had been able in the House to answer Disraeli himself, his anger would have found relief and the memory of those insults to his leader would have rankled less obstinately in his mind. But whereas when the deliberations began Gladstone had been in the House of Commons but out of the Government, he was now in the Government but out of the House of Commons. For when Peel reconstructed his Government in January 1846, he gave him the Colonial Office, the office Stanley had held before the party split. Gladstone had (as the law then stood) to resign, and failed to secure re-election. The Duke of Newcastle was a strong Protectionist, and Gladstone could not ask his tenants to support a Free Trader. As no other constituency could be found for him, Gladstone was a member of the Cabinet without a seat from January till June.[1] He did not return to

---

[1] The only similar instance since has been that of C. F. G. Masterman in 1914–15.

the House of Commons till August 1847. He was then elected for Oxford University, a seat that he retained with a steadily diminishing hold on the confidence of his constituents until 1865, when they rejected him.

Thus during his tenure of the Colonial Office, Gladstone was out of Parliament. His time was chiefly occupied with a scheme for settling 'exiles'—convicts who had served their sentences—in a new colony in North Australia. The scheme was dropped by his successor, though the practice of transportation of convicts continued for nearly twenty years more. A strong committee had reported adversely on it in 1837, though Darwin had found it not long before 'a means of making men outwardly honest,—of converting vagabonds most useless in one hemisphere into active citizens of another, and thus giving birth to a new and splendid country'; Gladstone seems to have inclined to Darwin's rather than to the committee's view. He was seriously interested in the possibilities of using transportation as a system of reform, but his ideas were too much in the air; moreover, he did not handle colonial opinion deftly enough. Opposition to him was headed in New South Wales by a Sydney barrister, Robert Lowe, who subsequently returned to England, defeated a more important project of Gladstone's in the reform debates of 1866, and then became Chancellor of the Exchequer in Gladstone's first Cabinet.

Gladstone's spell at the Colonial Office was short; for in repealing the Corn Laws, Peel had signed the death warrant of his Government. Peel resembled Pitt not only in his personal power but in his self-confidence, and as he had carried his Cabinet he expected to carry his party. But here he was sharply disillusioned. In the division on the second reading of the bill for repeal, over two hundred Conservatives followed Disraeli, and a few weeks later the Protectionists, putting their resentments before their principles, joined forces with the Whigs to defeat Peel on an Irish coercion bill. Peel had, in fact, destroyed for a generation the Conservative party that he had modernised and recreated as an effective force in politics. No Conservative Minister took office, with the strength in Parliament that had enabled Peel to play his great part in history, until Disraeli became Prime Minister in 1874.

It is not surprising that opinion has ever since been sharply divided on the moral and political merits and demerits of Peel's action. The predominant view is perhaps best expressed in Halévy's epigram that in 1832 the aristocracy surrendered political to preserve economic privileges and in 1846 surrendered economic to preserve political privileges. That was how Peel saw the choice before him in the winter of 1845. He thought that he was saving the nation by doing something that it wanted, and saving the aristocracy by doing something that it disliked. The Conservative party did not recover for a generation, but the revolutionary note of the forties went out of British politics.

Forty years later both Gladstone and Salisbury were guided in their behaviour on the Irish question by the lessons they learnt from these events.

Chapter Five

A Political Freelance
(1846–52)

THE division of the Conservative party over protection marked the start of a confused period in party history. Party boundaries were in any case uncertain, in an age when scores of members would go down to the House of Commons with open minds, and vote as the course of debate and the promptings of conscience, rather than the party whips, dictated. Members grouped themselves round particular leaders in support of general ideas, but permanent loyalties, either to men or to ideas, were comparatively rare. The Protectionist Conservatives were the largest single group in the Commons, but had to look for a leader, since they would not accept Disraeli, to Lord George Bentinck, a back-bench racehorse owner who disposed of his stud (and with it the coming winner of the Derby) and took to politics because, as he put it, 'what I cannot bear is being sold'. After Bentinck's death in 1848 the dearth of any other men of ability compelled the Protectionists to make Disraeli their leader, in the Commons, though they did not trust him.

At the general election held in 1847 the Protectionists carried two-thirds of the Conservative seats, numbering some 226 against about 105 followers of Peel. Whigs and Radicals together numbered about 325, so no party had a clear majority; but the Peelites supported Lord John Russell and his Whig Government, and this lasted over five years. During these years Gladstone was an independent member of Parliament. He was strongly attached to the person, and after 1850 to the memory, of Peel, and was specially intimate with Graham and Herbert, who had been his colleagues in Cabinet. But to most of his contemporaries he was an enigma, and to many a sinister enigma. He described himself in 1852 as preferring to be on the Liberal side of a Conservative party rather than on the Conservative side of a Liberal party; many of his public declarations were less explicit.

Pressure of family business took up at this time much of the attention that he would otherwise have devoted to politics. His wife's brother became involved in large liabilities in the financial crash of 1847, and Gladstone was much concerned in extricating him. The work introduced him in detail to the worlds of industry and business, and though it must have seemed tedious to him at the time 'it completed' —in Morley's words—'his knowledge of the customs, rules, maxims, and currents of trade and it bore good fruit in future days at the exchequer'. In the course of this settlement he bought much land in Flintshire, and as it came to be completed he and his wife settled in the house at Hawarden, west of Chester, where for centuries the Glynnes had had a family seat.

Yet he was not altogether inactive in politics. He displayed his liberalism in 1847 in a manner that showed that he put his principles before his interests, for his support of Lord John Russell's bill for removing Jewish disabilities, which outraged his father, had

54

the more serious consequence of displeasing many of his supporters at Oxford. He displayed his conservatism by resisting a proposal for a Commission to inquire into the affairs of the Universities. His overpowering interest in theology drew him into the heat of the battle over the doctrinal questions about baptism raised by the Gorham judgment in 1847. On these occasions he employed his remarkable talents for causes uncongenial to the liberal temperament. On the other hand, a great speech he made against Lord John Russell's Ecclesiastical Titles Bill in 1851 gave pleasure to Liberals at home and abroad, including Tocqueville the most eminent Liberal in France. The Pope had divided England into dioceses, and this step provoked violent agitation in which Protestant and John Bull sentiment combined. Russell shared the resentment, and fanned it into the last widespread outburst of 'No Popery' in English history. (His measure proved a dead letter, and Gladstone repealed it twenty years later.)

Gladstone's speech in this debate, in which the opponents of the bill mustered only 91 votes against 438, is described by Morley as one of his three or four conspicuous masterpieces. A sentence or two will give an impression of the large historical spirit in which he sought to combat the raging storm. He argued that it was undignified for Britain to abandon the principle of religious toleration which she had slowly and gradually adopted :

'Show, I beseech you— have the courage to show the pope of Rome, and his cardinals, and his church, that England too, as well as Rome, has her *semper eadem*; and that when she has once adopted some great principle of legislation, which is destined to influence the national character, to draw the dividing lines of her policy for ages to come, and to affect the whole nature of her influence and her standing among the nations of the world—show that when she has done this slowly, and done it deliberately, she has done it once for all; and that she will then no more retrace her steps than the river that bathes this giant city can flow back upon its source.'

Thirty years later, when religious intolerance shamefully exploited for factious purposes by Lord Randolph Churchill and his Fourth Party made a second Wilkes case out of Bradlaugh's unorthodox theology, Gladstone, as we shall see, faced ignoble passion in the same temper.

In two other spheres of politics Gladstone made a great advance during these years.

Tocqueville's famous book, *Democracy in America,* was published in 1836, and made a great impression on Gladstone, as it did on Peel. Tocqueville argued that the greater success of Britain as compared with France in founding colonies, and impressing her habits and traditions on North America, was due to her free institutions at home. This sank into Gladstone's mind, and at an early stage in his meditations on the problem he saw that the government of British colonies must be regulated by a sense of the value of freedom. On the other hand, Tocqueville's account of the inferior cultural condition of a people where taste was formed and regulated by persons unaccustomed to leisure led Gladstone to a conclusion that he fortunately discarded before he had gone much farther. This was that the mother country ought to provide the colonies with an established

Church and a landed aristocracy; a view that did not long survive his contact with facts.[1] He soon realised the difference between the social atmosphere of a new country and that of England, where the most powerful aristocracy in the world had consolidated its hold on all the institutions that served the purposes of government and culture. In a speech on the Government of Canada Bill in 1840, he found the real problem to be 'in what manner, and how long, shall we maintain a connexion between societies which, though still politically one, yet are not socially one?' Ten years later he had advanced to the full Liberal doctrine that Fox had declared in 1791 when speaking on Pitt's Quebec Bill: 'he was convinced that the only means of retaining distant colonies with advantage, was to enable them to govern themselves.' A speech Gladstone made on the New Zealand Bill in 1852 was printed by the group of colonial reformers led by Wakefield and Molesworth, and the same Liberal sentiments were well expounded three years later in a speech of his at Chester:

> '. . . experience has proved that if you want to strengthen the connexion between the colonies and this country . . . if you want to see British law held in respect and British institutions adopted and beloved in the colonies, never associate with them the hated name of force and coercion exercised by us, at a distance, over their rising fortunes. Govern them upon a principle of freedom. . . . Defend them against aggression from without—regulate their foreign relations (these things belong to the

[1] In 1791, Pitt, Burke, and Wilberforce all wanted to give Canada an hereditary aristocracy and an established Anglican Church. Fox objected to both.

colonial connexion, but of the duration of that connexion let them be the judges)—and I predict that if you leave them the freedom of judgment it is hard to say when the day will come when they will wish to separate from the great name of England. Depend upon it they covet a share in that great name. You will find in that feeling of theirs the greatest security for the connexion.'

It will be noted that in this speech Gladstone said that the regulation of the foreign relations of the colonies should remain in the hands of the British Government. The famous Durham Report [1] had drawn a distinction between matters in which the colony should have supreme power and those in which the mother country should keep control. Among the latter Durham included the constitution and the form of government; the regulation of foreign relations, and of trade with the mother country, the other British colonies, and foreign nations; and the disposal of public lands. Russell held that this division of power was impracticable. In the late forties the question came up again, and Gladstone with some friends supported the plan of separation. They called attention to the precedent of the Roman Empire and the constitution of the United States. These proposals came to nothing, owing to opposition within the Colonial Office, but the principle was revived a generation later in Gladstone's Home Rule Bills.

In this period the foundations were laid of the British Commonwealth of Nations, which came to

[1] Presented in 1839 by Lord Durham, who had been sent by Melbourne to Canada in the previous, and who died in the following, year. His report was the basis for the liberal policy adopted in 1846.

full growth in the Statute of Westminster in 1931. That development was made possible by the adoption of an imperial policy based on the ideas set out in Gladstone's speech at Chester in 1855. There Gladstone disclaimed the policy of holding the colonies by force or by the exercise of power over their internal arrangements. Strong free trader as he was, he rejected the temptation to thrust free trade upon them. His speeches laying stress on the community of sentiment and tradition as the true links between a mother country and its colonies, and the true ties of a commonwealth of free peoples, marked an important stage in his education as a Liberal.

Gladstone's speech on Russell's Ecclesiastical Titles Bill, described earlier in this chapter, showed how his developing European sense had drawn him out of a narrow circle of ideas on religion. A speech he made in 1850 on foreign affairs showed how that sense preserved him from the insular prejudices of his age. At Easter 1847 the house in Athens of a Mediterranean Jew name Pacifico, who claimed British citizenship because he had been born at Gibraltar, was sacked by a mob, angry that the usual ceremony of burning Judas Iscariot in effigy had been prohibited. Pacifico presented an exorbitant demand for compensation, which the Greek Government refused to satisfy. The British sent a fleet (larger than the fleet which Nelson had commanded at the Nile) to exact damages for this and other claims. Offers in London of French and Russian mediation were so mishandled that the French withdrew their ambassador. In June 1850 the House of Lords censured British policy on this issue, and a Commons debate was instigated to try to reverse the result. (In this

59

debate Peel delivered his last speech; next day he was thrown from his horse and fatally injured.) Palmerston, speaking 'from the dusk of one day to the dawn of the next', boasted that under his rule every Briton knew that, like a Roman citizen of old, he was safe from insult wherever he might find himself. Gladstone replied that the claims of Rome to a special status for her citizens were inconsistent with the equality of nations, and that it was invidious for a British Government to go beyond international law and arrogate special rights in virtue of its strength in a dispute with a weaker power. His speech defined the principles that governed his views of international relations for the rest of his life. Palmerston had nearly all the orators of the day against him, but his majority of 46 reflected a public opinion self-satisfied in British strength.

On both these occasions Gladstone defended liberal principles against nominally Liberal ministers, and the tone and passion of his oratory showed how close those principles were to his heart and conscience. In the winter of 1850 he passed through an experience that was to have a great influence on his future. His first visit to Italy, just after he left Oxford, had given him a new outlook on religion and emancipated him from his Evangelical servitude. In 1850 he paid another visit to Italy, with Mrs. Gladstone, with very important consequences. For he saw at close quarters the infamies of the rule of Ferdinand, the Bourbon King of Naples (nicknamed 'Bomba' after a bombardment and massacre at Messina in 1848).

What Gladstone saw that winter in Naples led him to describe the Bourbon regime there as 'the negation of God erected into a system of government'. That phrase would aptly describe other systems with which we have been familiar in recent times, but Bourbon rule contrasts favourably with them in one respect: Gladstone was allowed to visit the prisons freely and to observe the appalling conditions inside them. Gladstone found that the local Liberals thought that their persecution had been intensified because Palmerston's brother, the British Minister, had tried to intervene on their behalf; but they were anxious that this should not deter him from action. They said that the Neapolitan Government relied on the English Conservative party, and that they themselves had been alarmed when the vote of censure on Palmerston over the Pacifico incident had been carried in the Lords.

Gladstone came home in February 1851 to find an invitation waiting for him from Stanley to join the Conservative Cabinet that he was trying (without success) to put together after the defeat of Russell on a motion about reform of Parliament. Gladstone, full of the Naples horrors, had no mind to think of anything else, dismissed the idea of office, and went off to Aberdeen (who had been Peel's foreign secretary) to consult with him about the steps to be taken to bring pressure on Bomba's government. They agreed that private representations should be tried first. Aberdeen, though he was distressed by Gladstone's disclosures, differed from him in fundamental respects, for his devotion to the settlements of Vienna was as staunch as Metternich's, and he had criticised Palmerston for his Liberal interventions in Continental affairs. Months were consumed in dilatory proceedings between Aberdeen and various foreign diplomats.

At last Gladstone's patience gave out, and in July 1851 he published successively two *Letters to Lord Aberdeen* describing what he had seen at Naples. Aberdeen thought that Gladstone had not treated him fairly, but his note recording his regret pays full tribute to Gladstone's motives : 'I have certainly much reason to complain of Gladstone; but he is so honest and so perfectly sincere, and we are both personally and politically connected so closely, that although I have not concealed my feelings from him it is impossible for me to entertain any resentment.'

It is evident that nothing could have been done by the original method of private representation. Misunderstanding between Gladstone and Aberdeen was almost inevitable, for they wanted different things. Aberdeen wanted above all else to preserve the equilibrium set up by the Treaties of Vienna that had closed the great war in 1815—so far as that equilibrium had survived the shocks of 1848; Gladstone, Conservative though he was, wanted the drastic reform of such systems as that which he had watched in operation at Naples. His letters may have done the Italian Liberals harm in Italy, but certainly awakened feeling elsewhere in Europe. There was intense excitement in England; Palmerston congratulated Gladstone in the Commons, and circulated the letters to all British missions abroad for communication to other governments. They were translated into several languages.

The incident marked a definite step in Gladstone's advance towards Liberalism. It had also, later, a great effect on his views about democracy. His letters were really an appeal to the Conservatives of Europe.

Conservatives, he argued, as the supporters of established governments throughout the Continent, were under a special obligation to see that such abuses were corrected. The best of them were cold to his appeal. Others were abusive. Guizot, one of the most enlightened, sent Gladstone a long letter saying that the only choice was between tyrants and cut-throats, between the King of Naples and Mazzini, and he was for the King of Naples. A generation later Gladstone had an opportunity of noting the difference between popular audiences and the respectable and experienced Conservative statesmen of Europe. The arguments that fell on deaf ears when he appealed to the Guizots moved the working classes of England and Scotland to treat the Bulgarian atrocities as the most important question in public life, at a time when their own grievances were acute and the franchise had made them active citizens. Gladstone was European in his outlook in the fifties, but he was very far from being a democrat. His experiences in the Eastern agitation in the seventies taught him, as he told the Queen (to her horror), that 'on all the great questions dependent mainly on broad considerations of humanity and justice, wealth, station, and rank had been wrong and the masses right'. The letters to Lord Aberdeen, written in his middle years, thus helped in their results to make him a democrat in his old age.

At the end of 1851 an internal quarrel developed in the Government. Palmerston, the Foreign Secretary, defied the Cabinet's instructions in expressing approval to the French ambassador of Louis Napoleon's *coup d'état* of 2 December. For this Lord John Russell required him to resign. Palmerston's conduct had been irresponsible, but Russell had been tactless. Palmerston never forgave him, and three months later took revenge by organising a Government defeat in the Commons. Russell resigned in February 1852.

Chapter Six

The Crimean War Period
(1852–9)

LORD STANLEY (now Lord Derby) formed a Government with Disraeli as Chancellor of the Exchequer, but the general election that followed in the summer of 1852 did not confirm him in office, and he resigned at Christmas. The new House of Commons was made up of some 315 Liberals, 300 Conservatives, and 40 Peelites. After Peel's death, his followers had suffered the inevitable fate of a group which, distinguished though it was in quality, was too small in numbers to form an effective Government; yet it stood so high in prestige that it found itself in a remarkable position when a Government came to be put together. Russell, though a former Prime Minister and the leader of the largest party, could not form a Government because his quarrel with Palmerston had estranged a most powerful personality and his Ecclesiastical Titles Bill had made him obnoxious to the Irish. After a good deal of negotiation, Aberdeen formed a Government. He was a Peelite, and no less than six members of the new Cabinet of thirteen came from this small group; six of the other seven were Liberals and one, Sir William Molesworth, a Radical. Gladstone would have been glad to return to the Colonial Office, but when Sir James Graham refused the Chancellorship of the Exchequer, everybody looked to Gladstone as the right man for that office. Among others the Queen, later his bitter enemy, was particularly anxious that he should take it. So he accepted Aberdeen's invitation, and he made the Chancellorship what it remained for eighty-five years, the second place in the Government.

His work at the Board of Trade between 1841 and 1845 had made him eager to simplify and reorganise our fiscal system, and to relieve the poorer classes from the excessive burdens imposed on them by gross inequalities of taxation. In his first Budget in 1853 he applied the lessons he had learned as a Minister under Peel with such vigour and courage as to effect a fiscal revolution. He took off the tax on about 130 minor articles of food, abolished the soap tax, and reduced the tea duty by gradual stages to a shilling in the pound. It was now that he incurred for the first time the fierce hostility of the upper classes, a hostility that was to grow steadily throughout his career, so that when he left the world of politics the Whig aristocracy that had been so important an element in the Liberal party in 1832 was only represented in it by a handful of distinguished families. In 1796 Pitt had tried to extend the legacy duty on real property, but the landed interest had been too strong for him. Gladstone took up this project. The landed interest was not strong enough, as it proved, to defeat him, but it was strong enough to deter anybody but a man of exceptional courage from throwing down such a challenge. No other Minister of the time would have attempted it. Aberdeen told Nassau Senior that the whole Cabinet was against him when he proposed it, though he succeeded in converting every member.

Gladstone's first performance as Chancellor of the

Exchequer made a great impression at home and abroad. Greville wrote in his diary: 'It has raised Gladstone to a great political elevation, and, what is of far greater consequence than the measure itself, has given the Country the assurance of a *man* equal to great political necessities, and fit to lead Parties and direct Governments.' Senior, who was travelling on the Continent at the time, found that the boldness and comprehensiveness of the Budget astonished Frenchmen accustomed to the limited conceptions of national finance that ruled among French politicians. Cavour, who had lately begun his career as the First Minister of Victor Emmanuel, King of Sardinia and Piedmont, was full of admiration, and more than ever convinced that Italian statesmen should look to England for the best examples of political wisdom.

Gladstone unfolded in his first Budget a plan for the gradual reduction of the income-tax, but this scheme was upset by the outbreak of the Crimean War. Gladstone met the new war charges by doubling the tax; for he held that great disasters had been brought upon the country by excessive borrowing in the Revolutionary and Napoleonic Wars.

This is not the place to relate the complicated series of events that led up to the Crimean War; partly since it would range too far to weigh the influence of the ambitions of the Tsar Nicholas I, of the designs of Louis Napoleon, of the Turcophil tradition in the British diplomatic world, or of the popular detestation of the Tsar as a tyrant whose power was to be dreaded by every friend of freedom; and partly since Gladstone was not a member of the inner cabinet of five (Aberdeen, Clarendon, Graham, Palmerston, Russell), four of them at some time

Foreign Secretary, that dealt with the problems of diplomacy and the various and discordant forces of anti-Russian opinion.

Unhappily the Prime Minister was about the worst man to handle these forces. Aberdeen had been the Queen's choice. A writer of the time described what seemed to be his strongest qualification : 'With all the talents in one Cabinet, amenity is preferable to genius in the chief.' History was to falsify this view, as it was to illustrate the truth of another *obiter dictum* : 'The government of a harmless man is not necessarily a harmless Government.' Aberdeen was the only British statesman, besides Wellington (who had just died) and Lord John Russell, who had seen war at close quarters. As a young man he had been a useful diplomatic agent in the closing years of the Great War, and the sights of the Leipzig battlefield had haunted him ever since : 'I do not know when I have felt more severely the wretchedness of mankind.' Aberdeen had some admirable qualities—he was indeed one of the most honourable men who have ever taken part in politics—but it would probably have been better if any of the suggested alternatives —Palmerston, Derby, Russell, Clarendon, or Lansdowne—had been in his place when trouble began in the Near East.

Gladstone's attitude towards the Crimean War, as so often happened, defied all the familiar classifications. A speech that he made at Manchester in October 1853, which was praised by Aberdeen, gave the general tenor of his case. While he recognised the duty of maintaining the integrity and the independence of the Ottoman Empire, he insisted that the despotic rule of a Mohammedan power over twelve million Christians in Europe was an anomaly. This concern for the Balkan peoples distinguished his outlook from that of many supporters of the war. His view of their claims on Europe's sympathy was given in an unusually striking figure when in a speech he once compared the Balkan peoples to a shelving beach that restrains the ocean. 'That beach, it is true, is beaten by the waves; it is laid desolate; it produces nothing; it becomes perhaps nothing save a mass of shingle, of rock, of almost useless sea-weed. But it is a fence behind which the cultivated earth can spread, and escape the incoming tide, and such was the resistance of Bulgarians, of Servians, and of Greeks. It was that resistance which left Europe to claim the enjoyment of her religion, and to develop her institutions and her laws.'

Thus from the first Gladstone assumed the defence of the Balkan peoples as a mission. His support of the Crimean War did not imply any countenance of Turkish oppression. It represented his view, again a view that he held throughout his career, of the necessity of something like a system of public law in the life of Europe. Russia, in his opinion, was taking into her own hands a problem that ought to be solved, not by the arbitrary power of a strong and interested neighbour, but by common counsel and action. This view he held at the time, and he still held it over thirty years later when he discussed and defended the conduct of Aberdeen's Government in an article in the *English Historical Review* (April 1887).

If Gladstone defended the war on these definite principles, it was natural that he should cease to support it when those principles had been accepted. This was the position as he saw it in the spring of

1855, when negotiations had been opened and Russia had conceded almost all the demands of the Allies. Russia had surrendered the claim which Gladstone would not allow to an exclusive right of control in the Balkans, and a collective European guarantee was to be substituted for a Russian protectorate over Servia and the Roumanian principalities. The point on which the new Tsar, Alexander II, who had succeeded Nicholas in March, would not give way concerned Russia's position in the Black Sea, a point on which Gladstone never thought the Allies could sustain their claims against her.

By the time this difficulty was known, the Government had already broken up. It had not been successful in handling the problems of war. In the autumn of 1854 tales of soldiers ill clad, wounded ill cared for, and an incompetent command came back to England, and at the end of January 1855 Aberdeen's Government lost the confidence of the Commons and resigned. The prolonged and complicated crisis that ensued offered Gladstone a chance, which he refused, to re-enter the Conservative party under Derby, who also refused a chance to become Prime Minister in circumstances which could hardly have failed to bring his party popularity. Palmerston, popularly supposed to be the most anti-Russian Minister, eventually formed a Cabinet of Whigs and Peelites, which included Gladstone; but the latter with two friends (Graham and Herbert) resigned after three weeks on what seemed to everyone else to be a quibble about the relations of Cabinet and Parliament. Gladstone thus shared the unpopularity of Cobden and Bright, who had opposed the war all along, and was blamed by their pacifist supporters into the bargain for having supported it when it first broke out. *The Times,* whose revelations of conditions in the Crimea had precipitated the crisis, called 'the singular line Mr. Gladstone has selected . . . an unmitigated scandal'. He paid the penalty of having an intellect keen enough to discern, and a moral sense strong enough to assert, distinctions so fine as to be imperceptible to the ordinary man, in a temporary loss of standing in the eyes of the political public. This did not distress him. He spoke for peace in Parliament without effect, retired to Hawarden, and began to write a book on Homer.

The war went on for another year, and Russia had in the end to accept restrictions on her freedom in the Black Sea and wait for an opportune moment to be rid of them. This moment came with the Franco-Prussian War, so that of all the English statesmen responsible for the Crimean War it was Gladstone who suffered the worst consequences of the determination to force this demand upon the Tsar, for his wise proposal to mobilise neutral opinion for the defence of France against the seizure of Alsace-Lorraine in 1870 was largely defeated by Russia's need of Prussian support in putting an end to the restrictions that he had considered unjust and impracticable when they were imposed.

Politics were confused at this time because after Peel's Conservative opponents (under Disraeli's guidance) had abandoned protection the two parties were not divided by any question of principle. Personal feelings therefore counted more than they usually do in the conduct of public men. On several questions

Gladstone was still a Conservative, and his old party had strong hopes of his return. Offers were made to him in 1856 and 1858. On the second occasion Disraeli wrote a generous letter, to which Gladstone gave a cold and stiff reply. A fidgety conscience, strong personal loyalties, a mind with expanding interests in which old attachments and new and Liberal intuitions found it hard to live together, made the prospect of party harness uncongenial. What chiefly moved him and governed his oscillating and sometimes wayward behaviour during the next few years was his strong dislike of Palmerston's tone in international relations, a tone that he found imperious to the point of insolence. Palmerston has a great reputation as a Liberal Foreign Secretary, but before he went to the Foreign Office he had served under five Tory Prime Ministers, and Henderson—an acute critic—has observed that his 'viewpoint was fundamentally conservative'. He was a genuine humanitarian who often acted from generous motives, but he scoffed at all ideals for the future of humanity; and his support of 'constitutional' against 'despotic' powers abroad was largely due to suspicion of the despots' designs on British interests. His immense popularity was due to his assertions of British power when Great Britain was the most powerful nation on earth, not to any adherence to Liberal creeds; and as he got older, his true conservatism became more marked. Gladstone's dislike of him was balanced, however, by deep mistrust of Disraeli, a mistrust common to all the Peelites. But Palmerston was much more in touch with the electorate than his larger-minded adversary. This was shown clearly in the spring of 1857, when Palmerston dissolved Parliament after a defeat in the House of Commons in which Gladstone had played a part.

In the previous winter Sir John Bowring, the Governor of Hong-Kong, had resorted to violent measures in order to exact an apology from the local Chinese authorities for taking twelve Chinese, accused of piracy, from a ship with some claim to be British. The Chinese returned the men but refused the apology that Bowring demanded, and Bowring replied by bombarding Canton. When three months later news of these events came to London, a hostile motion of Cobden's was carried in the Commons by 263 to 247. On this occasion Gladstone and Disraeli both spoke on Cobden's side. Clarendon, Palmerston's Foreign Secretary, wrote that Gladstone's 'rabies for office renders him capable of anything', but the judgment was singularly wide of the mark on this occasion : Palmerston quoted against Gladstone in this very debate the intemperate expressions that had got him into trouble seventeen years earlier when he denounced the blockade of Canton 'for purposes at variance both with justice and with religion'. On no question was Gladstone's conduct more consistent, and one of his reasons for hesitating over Peel's offer of a Cabinet post in 1843 had been the fear that he might seem to approve of our treatment of China. In the Commons he made one of the most effective debating speeches of his life; but, in the country, Palmerston won a majority of nearly 100 at the general election which immediately followed. Cobden, Bright, and other opponents of the Crimean War lost their seats. (Gladstone was unopposed at Oxford.)

During the next few years Gladstone was in continual conflict with the national hero. His feeling that Great Britain was a member of a great community of nations, with obligations to a larger loyalty than the John Bull sentiment, so much alive and active at the time, was ready to recognise, was well illustrated in his differences with Palmerston on the question of the Suez Canal. The project of building this canal had been started by the French, and the British Government had used all its influence at Constantinople to dissuade the Sultan of Turkey (in whose dominions Suez still lay) from giving it his sanction. In 1857 and 1858 the subject was debated in Parliament. Gladstone argued in August 1857 that no man 'could look at the map of the globe, and deny that a canal through the Isthmus of Suez, if practicable, would be a great stroke for the benefit of mankind. . . . let us not create in Europe an opinion that the possession of India by Great Britain was something to be upheld by opposition to measures that were beneficial to the general interests of Europe'. Palmerston's reply included a typical sentence : 'It seems to me that if the British Government are of opinion that any scheme is injurious to British interests, it is their duty to oppose it, however much their opposition . . . may thwart the political and commercial wishes of any other country.' Ten months later Palmerston made another appeal to the House on grounds of confidence in the care shown by successive governments for 'the political and national interests of the country'. Gladstone, in 'a respectful but most serious protest', remarked that he was 'unwilling to set up the Indian Empire of Great Britain in opposition to the general interests of mankind, or to the general sentiment of Europe'.

By this time Palmerston was out of office, for in February 1858 he had suddenly found himself in a minority: the interpreter and representative of national spirit fell from power because he laid himself open to the charge of treating it with disrespect. Orsini, an Italian refugee in London, had planned an attempt on the life of Napoleon III. The Emperor escaped unhurt, but the bomb thrown at his carriage killed several bystanders. There was great indignation in France, and the French Minister for Foreign Affairs sent a rude dispatch demanding that Britain should discontinue her practice of harbouring criminal refugees (whether the Emperor, who was harboured in London for several years, would have come under this category might be a nice question). Palmerston did not answer the dispatch, but he introduced a bill which made conspiracy to murder a felony punishable with penal servitude, instead of a misdemeanour punishable only with a short term of imprisonment. This handling of the incident at a time when French invective had exasperated feeling in England was highly unpopular, and Palmerston was hooted in the park. Milner-Gibson proposed an amendment expressing the abhorrence of the House of the recent attempt in France and its readiness to amend defects in the criminal law, but censuring the Government for not replying to the dispatch from the French Foreign Secretary. Gladstone spoke in favour of this amendment, arguing that the French dispatch should have been answered and the principles of British law on the subject explained. To give this bill as an answer would have a grave effect on our position in the world and on the cause of liberty, a cause that was in great danger; it would attempt 'to establish a moral complicity between us and those who seek safety in repressive measures', and so it would 'be a blow and a discouragement to that sacred cause in every country in the world'. The amendment was carried by a majority of 19, and Palmerston thus left office under a reproach that nobody would have expected him to incur—that of being less high-spirited than the ordinary Englishman. The view that he had mishandled the affair and shown too little regard to Britain's character abroad received the support of 84 Liberals, with Lord John Russell at their head, of the Radical followers of Cobden and Bright, and also, outside the House of Commons, of so independent a critic as John Stuart Mill.

Palmerston resigned, and Derby formed a Government which held office till June 1859. During its short lifetime, Gladstone spoke on the Balkan principalities. Napoleon III had proposed that a Roumanian national State should be created by the union of the two Danubian principalities into a single State. The British Government joined Austria in opposing this suggestion. Meanwhile the provinces themselves declared in favour of the union by a plebiscite. Gladstone in a letter to Aberdeen put his own view more neatly than usual: 'I thought we made war in order to keep Russia out, and then suffer life, if it would, to take the place of death. But it now seems to be all but avowed, that the fear of danger, not to Europe, but to Islam—and [to] Islam not from Russia but from the Christians of Turkey,—is to be a ground for stinting their liberties.' In May 1858 he moved that the wishes of the people of Wallachia and Moldavia should be respected. Lord John Russell and Lord Robert Cecil, afterwards Lord Salisbury, supported him, but a large majority followed Palmerston and Disraeli, who spoke on the other side.

It was during the brief lifetime of the Derby Government that the Act which transferred the government of India from the East India Company to the Crown became law. Palmerston's Government had introduced a bill for this purpose just before its fall. In its original form the Derby bill contained some eccentric features, but the Act that finally emerged from long debates was the Act under which India was governed till the recent revolution. Gladstone, who had had some talks with Bright, was greatly impressed with the difficulties of the problem; he favoured the principle that 'India is to be governed for India and as far as may be proved practicable by India'. Twenty-two years later Ripon was sent to India by Gladstone to apply these principles as Viceroy. At the time, Gladstone made one important contribution to the new system. He persuaded the Government to accept his proposal that a provision should be inserted prohibiting the employment of the Indian Army outside India without the permission of Parliament—to afford, as he put it privately, 'a standing-ground from which a control might be exercised on future Palmerstons'.

In November 1858, Gladstone accepted an invitation from Bulwer-Lytton, the Colonial Secretary in Derby's Government, to go to the Ionian Islands, which had been put under a British protectorate in 1815. The islanders were anxious for union with Greece, and it was hoped that Gladstone might reconcile them to their continued connexion with Britain. Bulwer-Lytton described him as 'a statesman who belongs to his country rather than to any party, whose mind has grasped foreign as well as domestic questions with equal vigour and success, and whose renown as a Homeric scholar will justly commend him to the sympathies of an Hellenic race'. But these qualities, to which there had to be added the power of making eloquent speeches in faultless Italian, did not charm the islanders out of their fixed desire, even though Gladstone could promise them more self-government. Six years later Palmerston's Government gave the islanders what they wanted. Gladstone was then Chancellor of the Exchequer, and there was only one dissentient in the Cabinet (Lord Chancellor Westbury). Bismarck described the decision as 'a manifest symptom of British decadence'. Disraeli, in attacking it, said he hoped that the destinies of the British Empire were not going to be left to 'prigs and pedants'— curious terms to apply to Palmerston.

Gladstone's friends thought he had made a great mistake in accepting this hopeless mission, and he cannot have found much satisfaction from the result. But the enterprise had one consequence of importance : on his return journey he had a meeting with Cavour at Turin, on 23 March 1859. Events moved fast in the following weeks, both abroad and at home, and this talk doubtless confirmed Gladstone in the choice he had to make three months later.

At the end of March, Derby's Government was beaten on a Reform Bill in the Commons, and dissolved. The Conservatives gained a few seats in the general election, but not enough to give them a majority; meanwhile, on 29 April, the Austrians invaded Piedmont. On 3 May France entered the war on Piedmont's side, and under Napoleon's command French and Piedmontese troops won the battles of

Magenta and Solferino in June. Six days after Magenta, on 10 June, the new House of Commons defeated Derby's Government by 13 votes on a motion of confidence. Gladstone cast a silent vote on the Government side, but at once agreed to become Chancellor of the Exchequer in the new Cabinet which was formed by Palmerston. Thus he brought this phase of his career to an end by formal adhesion to the more liberal of the two great English parties.

Why did Gladstone take office under a statesman of whom he had been a most bitter and unsparing critic? Simply because the Italian issue had become the predominant one in the politics of western Europe. There had been little to distinguish Liberals from Conservatives in the fifties; whether Palmerston could work with Derby, or Graham with Disraeli, or Gladstone with either, depended much more on personal accidents than on large views of policy. But with the war for the liberation of Italy an issue emerged on which public men were drawn by their sympathies into opposite camps. The Conservatives were Austrian in sympathy. (Disraeli himself was so hostile to the Italian cause that he refused to meet Garibaldi when he came to England in 1864.) On the other hand, Palmerston, Russell, and Gladstone, who had been kept apart by principles and personal feeling, now found themselves in whole-hearted agreement. Gladstone's decision was sharply criticised, for only a week elapsed between his vote for Derby and his joining Palmerston. Yet he had voted for Derby in hopes of a Derby-Palmerston coalition, which would have excluded the most pro-Austrian Conservatives; and when Derby fell, and no coalition could be formed, there was no reason why he should think it wrong to give Palmerston's Whiggish Cabinet his full support and adherence. On the contrary, he knew that if he joined Palmerston and Russell the three of them could afford powerful support to the Italian cause. For such an object he was ready to put old prejudice aside, and as he wrote to Acton some years later—'the overwhelming interest and weight of the Italian question, and of our foreign policy in connexion with it, joined to my entire mistrust of the former government in relation to it, led me to decide without one moment's hesitation'.

Chapter Seven

Gladstone and Palmerston
(1859–67)

WHEN Gladstone entered Palmerston's Government in 1859 he was regarded as a man of mystery. When Palmerston died in 1865, Gladstone still retained some of his Conservative opinions, and he made speeches from time to time that ruffled or frightened Liberals. But he had emerged as the Liberal leader of the future. For in these years he had been the spokesman of Liberal and democratic views against Palmerston's resistance to reform. The conflict between the two had been animated and almost unremitting. The letters later published by Guedalla, in which they exchanged arguments, provide a most interesting study in contrasts of character, outlook, and beliefs.

On one large question they were in agreement, the question of immediate importance. Gladstone's decision to join Palmerston and Russell in order to befriend the Italian cause was needed to turn the scale, for they had against them all the influence of the Court, and the Cabinet was in the main lukewarm or adverse. Granville, who was highly critical of their proceedings, lamented the great moral force created by the combination of three powerful men who had spent most of the last ten years in thwarting one another.

Napoleon III, more alarmed by success than his uncle had been by defeat, astonished the world by making the preliminary peace of Villafranca on 11 July. Trevelyan describes in his *Garibaldi and the Thousand* the motives of this sudden decision. Prussia was considering plans for invading France, Russia had been upset by the spectre of revolution in Europe, at home in France the Clericals were becoming more and more hostile. Trevelyan puts it that Napoleon 'determined to avoid his Leipzig and Waterloo while there was yet time.' But the terms of peace sadly tarnished the credit he had won by his knight-errant adventure. Not only was Austria left in possession of Venetia, but the old ducal and papal despotisms were restored in Tuscany, Modena, and Romagna. All that had been done towards rebuilding Italy was the expansion of Piedmont by the inclusion in that kingdom of Lombardy.

From this unpromising situation Italy emerged in 1861 a single monarchy embracing the whole of the peninsula except for Venetia and Rome, consolidated by a series of plebiscites in which the Two Sicilies as well as the northern states and duchies had declared for union. Victor Emmanuel's common sense, Cavour's very uncommon sense, and Garibaldi's military leadership could not have secured this triumph had it not been for the three men who controlled British policy in these years. All the other great powers were hostile. Prussia and Russia would have welcomed, and aided by their diplomacy, the reconquest of Lombardy by Austria. Napoleon would have deplored such a setback, but he did not favour Cavour's larger ambitions, for he did not want Italy to be strong enough to be a possible rival to France.

He tried to persuade Russell to agree that the British and French fleets should be sent to Messina to prevent Garibaldi from crossing to the mainland after his sensational victories in Sicily. But Russell refused, guided by advice from Hudson our Minister at Turin, and thereby retrieved a reputation that had lost some of its bloom since the days of the great Reform Bill.

It looked at one time as if Italy's liberation might be wrecked by a quarrel between the two powers that were most friendly to it. The bargain struck between Cavour and Napoleon at their famous meeting at Plombières in July 1858 had included among its terms the cession of Nice and Savoy to France. When in the spring of 1860 effect was given to this promise, there was an outburst of indignation and suspicion in England. Palmerston himself was in such a temper that Trevelyan thinks that if his Government had been, like that of 1856, a Palmerston dictatorship, war would have followed. Fortunately the Government was not a dictatorship : it was, so far as Italian affairs were concerned, a triumvirate, and one of the triumvirs was Gladstone. All his influence was used now to counteract the impulsive recklessness of his two colleagues.

Gladstone had already done something to combat the excessively harsh view that had been taken of Napoleon's conduct in making the peace of Villafranca. In a Cabinet memorandum of 3 January 1860, he reminded his colleagues that Napoleon had a case. 'When . . . we fling in his face the truce of Villafranca, he may reply—and the answer is not without force—that he stood single-handed in a cause when any moment Europe might have stood combined against him.' His British critics were apt to overlook the great risks that Napoleon ran in embarking on the Austrian war, an adventure in which Britain had given him sympathy but no military aid. Gladstone went on to say that the alliance with France was the true basis of peace in Europe for England, and France would never engage in any European purpose which was radically unjust.

In March 1860 the storm of indignation over Nice and Savoy carried Russell away as well as Palmerston, although he had been convinced by Hudson that Cavour was right to make his bargain with Napoleon, hard as some of its terms might be. On 26 March he made a vehement speech in the Commons, in which he suggested that the French nation, its appetite once whetted by plunder, would demand from its Government further satisfactions of the same sort. Palmerston told his friend Count Flahault to let the Emperor know that Russell's speech represented his own opinion, and when Flahault said, 'C'est la guerre', Palmerston replied, 'Eh bien, si c'est la guerre, c'est la guerre. Que voulez-vous?' It is not surprising that Austria derived hope and comfort from this unexpected speech, which provoked an immediate response. The Austrian ambassador was instructed to explain to Russell that Austria was ready to enter into a treaty with Great Britain to resist any further encroachments on her territories; but Russell drew back, for he saw the trap into which he was to be drawn. He replied that neither the Government nor the people of Great Britain would ever sanction a war to support the authority of the King of the Two Sicilies (Bomba) against the just discontent of his subjects.

Gladstone did not merely combat the extravagant

suspicions that Napoleon's conduct had excited in the minds of Palmerston and Russell. He took active steps to improve the relations of the two countries. The success of Peel's policy and the great impression made on the Continent by Gladstone's brilliant budget had turned Napoleon III to the ideas of free trade. In the autumn of 1859 Cobden had visited Gladstone at Hawarden, and suggested that, as he was going to spend some part of the winter in Paris, he might be of use to the Cabinet as an informal envoy, to discuss the idea of a commercial treaty between the two countries with the Emperor and his Ministers. Palmerston and Russell were both doubtful, but Gladstone persuaded them to let Cobden try his hand. Cobden, who proved a most persuasive diplomat, achieved a great success after some arduous months of discussions and negotiation in Paris. But there were hostile influences to be encountered at home. The income-tax payer would have to make up for the fall in revenue caused by the proposed ending of duties on light French wines, and if the exporting industries of northern England gained by the treaty, some other English manufacturers might expect a more formidable French invasion of their markets. *The Times* said that 'a very finished effort of oratory' would be required to reconcile country squires, professional men of all classes, silk weavers, and English clockmakers to such sacrifices for doubtful advantage. Gladstone supplied the very finished effort : 'He came forth', Greville wrote, 'and consensu omnium achieved one of the greatest triumphs that the House of Commons ever witnessed.'

In a letter to his wife Gladstone described the Treaty as a great European operation. He said much later that 'the choice lay between the Cobden Treaty and not the certainty, but the high probability, of a war with France'. That is how both he and Cobden regarded it. Cobden bitterly resented Russell's behaviour in making a violent anti-French speech while he was in the thick of his business, and wrote to Bright asking him to put a stop to any proposal to vote him a public grant for his services.

The Italian success was a great achievement for British diplomacy: Trevelyan has compared it with the successful handling of the Belgian Revolution in 1831. But it was a solitary success, for the problems created by the rise of new forces and new men in Europe and across the Atlantic demanded in those who had to meet them more knowledge, statesmanship, and foresight than were to be found in British politicians. Italy was the one country of which the leading Ministers in the Palmerston Government had intimate knowledge, either from personal experience, as in Gladstone's case, or from the counsel of exceptionally qualified agents, as in Russell's. In the series of disturbances that followed, British Ministers were less happily placed.

The first of these was the American Civil War. Of the politicians of the time, Bright was the spokesman of those for whom slavery was the leading issue; his speeches on this subject were among the noblest he ever made, and would by themselves have given him lasting fame. The war, it is true, was maintained for a year and a half before slavery was made a direct issue by Lincoln, but for the plain man it was obvious from the first that a Southern victory would mean, in fact, a victory for slavery, with consequences to the world of incalculable gravity. Yet the English upper classes disliked the temper and politics of the North, and their dread of American democracy coloured their views of the struggle.

There were moments when it looked as if Great Britain and the United States might come to an open quarrel. The first danger arose in December 1861 when two Southerners, Mason and Slidell, sent to Europe for propaganda purposes, were taken from a British ship and carried as prisoners into a Northern port. America, having gone to war in 1812 to contest the overbearing claims made by Britain as a naval power, was now asserting those claims herself. The Cabinet decided to send a stiff dispatch. At the meeting which considered it, Gladstone was in a minority that favoured more moderate language. The situation was saved by the Prince Consort, then rapidly sinking (he died a fortnight later), who made some suggestions that were accepted by Palmerston and Russell. The particular point on which Gladstone had been anxious for reconsideration was the proposal to tell Lyons, our Minister in Washington, that he was to return if the British demands were not accepted in seven days. Russell seems to have come round to Gladstone's view, for he sent a private note to Lyons instructing him to say that he desired to abstain from anything like menace. Bright and Cobden helped the cause of peace by writing to their friend Charles Sumner, Chairman of the Senate Foreign Affairs Committee : 'At all hazards', wrote Bright, 'you must not let this matter grow to a war with England.' The two men were released.

The blame for the second crisis falls on Russell, though he was partly the victim of accidents. In June 1862 Adams (the American Minister) warned him that a ship then in course of construction at Birkenhead was intended for use as a Confederate privateer. The Commissioners of Customs whom Russell consulted replied that there were not sufficient grounds to warrant the detention of the vessel. Adams contested this view, and sent Russell additional documents, which were referred to the Law Officers. It happened that the Queen's Advocate, to whom they went first, had just gone out of his mind, though the Foreign Office was unaware of his condition. Thus some time was wasted before the documents reached the Attorney-General and Solicitor-General, on whose decision everything turned. They came quickly to the same conclusion as Adams, and Russell acted on their report at once. While his telegram ordering the arrest of the vessel was on its way to the port, the ship set sail—ostensibly for a trial run—and never returned.

Russell, awake to the tremendous mischief that had been done, wanted to give orders for her to be seized if she touched at any British port, but the Lord Chancellor declared that this would be a breach of law. For the next two years the *Alabama,* as the ship was named, with a crew largely British, plundered Northern merchantmen and excited most bitter feeling in America against us. The consequences of the negligence of the British authorities lasted for years after the war was over. The American Government, inheriting Lincoln's victory without his wisdom, prolonged the tension by making ludicrously extravagant claims for compensation, which provoked their best friend, Bright, to indignant remonstrance. It fell to Gladstone to compose this long quarrel. As Prime Minister ten years later, he made some reparation for his egregious misunderstanding of the American problem in 1862 in the third crisis by his courageous fidelity to the principle of arbitration under most difficult conditions and at the cost of much popularity.

This third crisis was caused by Gladstone himself. In the earlier part of 1862 the war went badly for the North, though the Northern blockade of Southern ports was doing great damage to British and French industries. Both Palmerston and Russell thought that the time might have come for offering mediation. Napoleon III, busy with his fatal schemes for a Mexican empire, was in touch with the Southern states through Slidell, and in July he received from Jefferson Davis, the Southern President, an offer of help in Mexico and the delivery of a large quantity of cotton. Napoleon tried to draw Great Britain into his plans, but both Palmerston and Russell were suspicious and held back. After the great defeats of the Northern armies in August, they began to think more seriously of trying to get a joint offer of mediation from Britain, France, and Russia. Gladstone favoured these ideas, partly because he was concerned about the effects of cotton famine and resulting unemployment on the working men of Lancashire,[1] but much more strongly because he was appalled by the ferocity of the war and its casualties, and feared that if the two sides fought each other to a standstill the result would be good neither for free institutions in the North nor for the slaves in the South.

Unfortunately, at a banquet at Newcastle in October he lost his head and made a notorious declaration about Jefferson Davis, which he well de-

---

[1] During the autumn of 1862 a thousand workpeople a day were fed under Mrs. Gladstone's care.

scribed afterwards as 'a mistake . . . of incredible grossness'. 'There is no doubt', he declared, 'that Jefferson Davis and other leaders of the South have made an army; they are making, it appears, a navy; and they have made what is more than either, they have made a nation.' It would be difficult to find an outburst harder to defend. The inference that the Government were about to recognise the South was irresistible. Adams told Russell that if he had trusted to the construction given by the public to the speech, he would have begun to think about packing his trunks. Russell sent a polite rebuke to his colleague : 'you must allow me to say that I think you went beyond the latitude which all speakers must be allowed, when you said that Jeff. Davis had made a nation. Recognition would seem to follow, and for that step I think the cabinet is not prepared.'

In November, Napoleon made a formal proposal to the British Cabinet to mediate, with a threat of force to both sides if necessary, to end the war; but Gladstone was almost alone in giving it serious countenance. Meanwhile Derby and Disraeli had done the country a great service by letting Palmerston know that they could not pledge themselves to support the Government if its proceedings led to hostilities. Any possibility of a mediation, which would have been to the advantage of the South, retreated from view when Lincoln issued his famous proclamation declaring that all slaves in the rebellious states were free. That proclamation had an immediate and powerful effect on British opinion, which veered in favour of the North, and Gladstone made no further efforts for mediation.

The Ministers who had done so well in the case of

Italy and so badly in that of the Civil War were unhappy in their handling of other European affairs. In two cases they took a tone that they could not sustain, and incurred all the discredit that descends upon unsuccessful bluff. In 1863 they came to grief over Poland, in 1864 over Denmark. In the first case there was vehement public feeling in England about the behaviour of the Russians in imposing conscription on the Poles by a gross abuse of the law, and then repressing the insurrection they provoked by terrible cruelty. Russell in the course of discussions on the question went so far as to suggest that 'representative institutions' should 'be granted at one and the same time to the kingdom of Poland and to the Empire of Russia'; thinking apparently that the Tsar was no more formidable than King Bomba, for whose edification he had written a famous sermon in 1860. As it happened, the Tsar had behind him the most powerful man in Europe. Bismarck not only aided him in putting down the insurrection, but for his own purposes fomented the Tsar's vindictive temper against the Poles.

In the case of Denmark, Palmerston announced (without consulting his Cabinet) that if 'certain Powers' attacked Denmark it would not be Denmark alone with which they would have to contend. The history of the quarrel between Denmark and Prussia is long and complicated. There was a point when Russell's efforts to negotiate a compromise were rendered more difficult by the unreasonable temper of the Danes. But Bismarck wanted something more than a compromise over the disputed provinces of Slesvig-Holstein, and he laid deliberate plans for the aggrandisement of Prussian power. When those plans were mature and the war he wanted came, Denmark found herself without an ally, and England, with Palmerston's threat fresh in her memory, had to look on in sullen silence while Bismarck enforced his will.

These unpleasant experiences brought great discredit on Palmerston's methods. The truth was that a new era had begun in Europe. Nobody understood yet, or for some time to come, the power of Bismarck or its effects on Continental politics. Disraeli, who had been wiser than Ministers about America, was no quicker than anybody else to appreciate the change in the balance of forces. The French were equally blind. Most French politicians, including Napoleon III, wanted to see Prussia stronger, for they thought Austria the chief danger in Europe. This illusion was strangely persistent. It is then not surprising that the Liberal Ministers misjudged this new force, though it seems almost incredible that so late as January 1864 Palmerston could have described the man who was soon to be Europe's new master as 'struggling in the torrent and crying out for help from some friendly hand'.

The British Ministers found their villain and bogy elsewhere. Palmerston never forgot that he had served at the War Office during the great war against the great Napoleon; more recently, he and Russell were still nursing the suspicions with which the lesser Napoleon had filled their minds when he took Savoy and Nice. Napoleon III was an enigma. He is one of the best illustrations of the difficulty of realising the maxim of Phocylides that a man should first acquire a competence and then practise virtue. He had some large humanitarian ideas. Indeed, his unpopularity in France after his fall was aggravated by resentment on this ground : it was thought that he had aimed too much at being a good European, and sacrificed in pursuit of that aim the interests of France. But the idealist looking to the future was from time to time surprised by the conspirator created by his past. The methods by which he had acquired power would suddenly reappear when he was using it. So the man whose head was full of ideas of nationality and European congresses would from time to time revert to the sharper and the knave.

It is clear that nothing could have checked Bismarck in his designs on Denmark, or prevented the oppression of Poland, but that Anglo-French alliance which Gladstone had described as the best basis for peace. Unhappily such co-operation was rendered impossible by Palmerston's suspicion of the French. Very serious results followed from this unhappy chapter of British diplomacy. Bismarck was able to do a wrong to Denmark, Prussia and Russia became allies, France was dangerously weakened, and Britain lost almost all her political influence in a world dominated by Bismarck's will and Bismarck's power.

What was Gladstone's part in this process? What was his responsibility for the condition to which Europe and British influence in it had been reduced? He was fighting all these years, with Cobden's and Disraeli's support, against Palmerston over military and naval expenditure. Napoleon had proposed a naval agreement to Palmerston in 1849, before he had proclaimed himself Emperor, and during the Crimean War he had made it clear that he was ready to leave British supremacy at sea unchallenged. Palmerston's military and naval expenditure was, nevertheless, directed against France, the one power with whose help we might have checked Bismarck. Gladstone was thus contending against a panic that was at once groundless and mischievous. If in the course of Palmerston's last Government Bismarck was able to take the first effective steps in establishing his power, the chief cause was Palmerston's fear of Napoleon. Gladstone did his best to combat that fear. Nobody now would deny that, on the question of danger from France, Gladstone and Cobden were right and Palmerston wrong.

In Gladstone's early days as a Liberal, Disraeli taunted him with the famous speech he made as an undergraduate at the Oxford Union, attacking the great Reform Bill on high Tory principles. Gladstone replying contrasted himself with Russell, a lifelong Liberal and trusted as such, and compared his own case to that of Aeneas cast ashore by the storms of the sea and welcomed by Dido. 'I came among you an outcast from those with whom I associated, driven from them, I admit, by no arbitrary act, but by the slow and resistless forces of conviction. I came among you, to make use of the legal phraseology, *in forma pauperis*. I had nothing to offer you but faithful and honourable service. You received me, as Dido received the shipwrecked Aeneas—*ejectum littore, egentem Excepi*—and I only trust you may not hereafter at any time have to complete the sentence in regard to me—*et regni demens in parte locavi*.[1] You received me with kindness, indulgence, generosity, and I may even say with some measure of confidence.'

[1] 'I took him in when he was cast up in need on my shore; and was mad enough to let him stay in my kingdom.' —Virgil, *Æneid* IV, 373-4.

This picture of Gladstone's welcome by the Liberal party is pleasant but misleading. The Liberals in the House of Commons had no great liking for him or, so far as they could understand them, for his views. Like his great antagonist, he found his way to the first place by making himself indispensable. Graham had said of him, referring to his intellectual power : 'He must rise to the head in such a government as ours, even in spite of all the hatred of him'. Disraeli described him to Northcote in 1866 as a man of transcendent ability who could not deal with men. To understand what happened to him between 1859 when he joined Palmerston's Government and 1868 when he became Prime Minister, we must remember that, so far as liking and understanding went, the Liberal party in the House of Commons gave its heart and confidence to Palmerston and not to Gladstone.

The two men, the old leader and the future leader, were in constant conflict on almost all domestic topics. They differed on armaments, on taxation, and on parliamentary reform. In 1860 Palmerston opposed one of Gladstone's pet projects. The Budget of 1860 was so drastic that Gladstone could say afterwards that it left on the Statute Book no protective duty of more than nominal amount; but one of its proposals was defeated in the Lords. Gladstone wanted to take off the excise duty on paper. He expected several benefits from this reform, among them the cheapening of books and papers. Palmerston was hostile, and spoke in that sense for three-quarters of an hour in Cabinet. He felt so strongly on the subject that he told the Queen that the House of Lords would do good service in rejecting the proposal. It is not surprising, therefore, that when the Lords threw out the

Paper Duties Bill, Palmerston's public criticisms of their actions were lukewarm. The Cabinet agreed on certain resolutions of protest, but Palmerston in moving them was described by a friend of Gladstone's as 'moving resolution condemnatory of the Lords, and yet speaking in defence of their conduct'.

The action of the Lords in 1860 had a momentous consequence. In the following year, after a struggle in Cabinet, Gladstone made an innovation in the form in which the Budget proposals were submitted to the Lords. Hitherto a number of separate bills had gone to the Lords, but on this occasion Gladstone collected all his tax provisions in a single bill, so that the Lords had either to reject or to swallow them all. This method has been customary ever since. By this device Gladstone confirmed the supremacy of the House of Commons in finance, a supremacy that went unchallenged until 1909, when the House of Lords was rash enough to throw out Lloyd George's Budget with results disastrous to itself, for the Parliament Act of 1911, reducing its power of control over legislation of every kind, was the result of the peers' temerity. If Gladstone had not defeated the Lords in 1861 and secured the recognition of the paramount rights of the Commons, Harcourt's great Budget of 1894 would have brought on a fierce struggle between the two Houses. Thus, apart from the other merits of his performance as Chancellor of the Exchequer, he must be given credit for a vindication of democracy, which added immensely to the strength and prestige of popular government in Britain.

Palmerston had no taste for such triumphs. His general attitude to domestic reform is illustrated by what he said in February 1864 to Goschen, a young banker new to the House of Commons, when instructing him how to outline Government policy at the opening of the session. Palmerston ran through a number of points on foreign policy, and added in reply to the question of what was to be said about domestic matters : 'there is really nothing to be done. We cannot go on adding to the Statute Book *ad infinitum*. Perhaps we may have a little law reform, or bankruptcy reform; but we cannot go on legislating for ever'. One kind of reform in particular Palmerston disliked, and that was any extensive parliamentary reform. Gladstone had made up his mind in favour of an extension of the franchise before he joined the Government. Lord John Russell also wanted reform. Unfortunately there was not much drive behind the demand in the country.[1] Russell had brought in a bill in the first year of the Government, but it was killed by apathy in the House of Commons and the country alike.

Before Palmerston's last Government went out of office, Gladstone had done a great deal to dissipate this apathy and to awaken working-class feeling on the franchise. At this time he learned some important lessons. The Civil War on which he had made such unhappy blunders had taught him, as he said afterwards, the power of political democracy. In the great war with France, Fox had argued that the strength

[1] In March 1861 Cobden wrote: 'I wonder the working people are so quiet under the taunts and insults offered them. Have they no Spartacus among them to head a revolt . . ? I suppose it is the reaction from the follies of Chartism, which keeps the present generation so quiet. . . . The middle class have never gained a step in the political scale without long labour and agitation out of doors, and the working people may depend on it they can only rise by similar efforts, and the more plainly they are told so the better.'

that Revolutionary France had discovered in fighting for her existence showed the power of democratic ideas, and he drew the moral that Parliament should pass a reform bill and give Britain similar vitality. Gladstone drew the same moral from the success of the North in the Civil War; a demonstration of will and energy to which he could find no parallel. (Salisbury drew the opposite moral from the conduct of the politicians of the North in exploiting the South after victory.) That war had also revealed in the working class at home qualities that showed its fitness for the franchise : the fortitude of the Lancashire textile workers in the sufferings they endured from the Northern blockade, and their sympathy with the Government that inflicted these hardships upon them because they held its cause to be just.

Gladstone had also come into touch with working-class leaders. In 1864 he had an amicable talk with a deputation from the London Trades Council which supported a measure of his for the sale of annuities through the Post Office. During this talk the trade unionists said that the working classes were dissatisfied with the parliamentary suffrage. Gladstone suggested that if Parliament had been inactive, it was partly because the working classes had seemed to be indifferent. This conversation later had an effect outside Parliament. In 1866 the Council, which in 1861 and 1862 had refused to take any interest in the subject, took a leading part in the agitation for reform.

It is not surprising that Gladstone in this mood soon upset his chief. In May 1864 Gladstone was to speak for the Government about a bill to extend the franchise, and Palmerston warned him against giving any pledges for the future. Gladstone made a statement that excited immense enthusiasm among the Radicals and the working-class leaders, and corresponding horror among the Whigs and Conservatives. He said : 'I venture to say that every man who is not presumably incapacitated by some consideration of personal unfitness or of political danger is morally entitled to come within the pale of the Constitution.' He added at once a caution : 'Of course, in giving utterance to such a proposition, I do not recede from the protest I have previously made against sudden, or violent, or excessive, or intoxicating change'. This reservation was accompanied by a series of characteristic qualifications and refinements, and anybody who read and studied the whole speech as an exercise might have concluded that the sentence that stood out had been explained away. But it was not to be expected that the public would treat the speech as a scholar would treat a passage in Plato or Thucydides. That sentence took hold of the popular imagination, and Gladstone became the hero of the reformers. Disraeli fastened on it and said Gladstone had revived the doctrines of Tom Paine. Bright wrote to his wife : '*The Times* is wroth with him this morning, and he will be more than ever the dread of the aristocratic mob of the West End. . . . I think the political prospect is brighter than for some time.'

Palmerston wrote to Gladstone at once to complain, with great good temper, on two reasonable grounds. His first objection was of course to the flagrant sentence. The second was that in the course of his speech Gladstone told the story of the deputation from the London Trades Council. Palmerston held that for a Minister to tell working men that the belief that the working classes were indifferent to the extension of the franchise was one of the causes of the inaction of Parliament was virtually an exhortation to them to agitate. Gladstone, who could be blinder than anybody else when he liked, replied that he could not see how Palmerston could put such a construction upon his language. He went on to assure Palmerston that the best thing he could do was to publish the speech, and proceeded to do so; though Palmerston thought this would only make things worse. Gladstone added a preface, which even his warmest friends found obscure. But there was nothing obscure in the speech for the working men and the reformers. Gladstone now shared their loyalty with Bright.

In October 1865, just short of his eighty-first birthday, Palmerston died. Russell, who had gone to the Lords in 1861, succeeded him as Prime Minister, and Gladstone became the Leader of the Commons. A new Parliament had been elected in the summer. It was slightly more Liberal than its predecessor (some 367 Liberals to 290 Conservatives), but it was less liberal in its attitude to parliamentary reform than either Russell or Gladstone. This soon became evident when Gladstone introduced a reform bill reducing the property franchise qualification and giving the vote to lodgers paying £10 a year. Robert Lowe, who had formed a very unfavourable view of democracy in Australia, where he had lived from 1842 to 1850, led a successful revolt. The second reading of the bill was only carried by a majority of 5 (with 32 Liberals in the minority), and one of the Adullamites, as Lowe's party were nicknamed by Bright,[1] carried an amendment substituting rating for rental in fixing the fran-

---

[1] 1 Samuel xxii. 1–2.

chise qualification. Gladstone opposed the amendment on two grounds : it would give assessors of rates control over suffrage, and it would much diminish the number of new voters. The number that would be enfranchised by the Government bill was itself smaller than Gladstone wanted, and as the debates developed his Liberalism became steadily warmer. A question asked by Lowe—whether if you wanted venality, ignorance, drunkenness, and impulsive, unreflecting, violent people, you went to the top or to the bottom —provoked one of his famous outbursts. He hit off the temper of such bitter opponents when he said that they handled the statistics of the bill as if they were ascertaining the numbers of an invading army, rather than considering the claims of 'our fellow-Christians, our own flesh and blood'.

The Russell Government resigned on this defeat in June 1866, and Derby became Prime Minister, with Disraeli Chancellor of the Exchequer and Leader of the House of Commons. The next few months produced a reform that added to the electorate not 400,000 but nearly a million voters. This was an astonishing sequel to the destruction of the more moderate measure as dangerously democratic. It was due to two things, the great manifestation of reform sentiment in the country and Disraeli's extraordinary skill and audacity as a parliamentary tactician.

Just before the general election of 1865 Denison, the Speaker, said that there was very little feeling about reform in the country. The debates that ended in the resignation of Russell's Government put an end to that apathy. A week after its resignation a huge procession marched to Gladstone's house to cheer the fallen Ministers, and next month the railings round

Hyde Park were pushed down by a vast crowd which had assembled for a reform meeting. There were similar demonstrations in Edinburgh, Glasgow, Manchester, Birmingham, Leeds, and other large cities. In the country at large, Gladstone and Bright were the heroes of the agitation. Gladstone was, indeed, given more credit than he deserved, for while Bright delivered a series of brilliant speeches, Gladstone, much hurt by his treatment at the hands of Liberals in the House of Commons, spent a sulky winter in Rome. He told Brand that he would leave the 'wound of the Liberal party to the healing powers of nature'.

The exhibition of strong feeling in the country was one force in producing household suffrage out of a House of Commons in which the friends of reform were in a minority. The other force was the genius of Disraeli. Like Gladstone, he was unpopular and mistrusted in his own party, but he was as skilful as Gladstone was unskilful in handling men. In the next few months he showed himself a master of parliamentary tactics.

For over a year there had been something like friendship between Disraeli and Bright. They were drawn together because both of them resented the patrician prejudices of the two parties. A Conservative describing Disraeli to Harcourt said : 'we know he does not belong to our eleven, but we have him down as a professional bowler.' Bright's unlimited self-confidence, which gave him his force in a House of Commons dominated by his enemy Palmerston, repelled even admirers of his eloquence. Morley said it amounted to 'corruption of the soul'. The two men met in the Lobby on 1 March 1867, and had some talk about the reform question. Encouraged by Disraeli's tone, Bright sent him a confidential paper arguing that by adopting household suffrage Disraeli could put an end to the agitation. Disraeli had been reluctant to take up reform in the winter when Derby had been pressing it, but he now caught at the hope of gaining for himself and his party the credit of settling this troublesome question. A year before he had denounced Gladstone's £7 qualification on the ground that it would produce 'a Parliament of selfish and obscure mediocrities, incapable of anything but mischief and that mischief devised and regulated by the raging demagogue of the hour'. But Disraeli never allowed himself to be embarrassed by inconvenient memories, and he had never been at heart opposed to household suffrage. He took Bright's advice, and by a combination of craft and courage he succeeded in making a lukewarm House of Commons pass a bill on Bright's lines.

He brought in a bill for household suffrage subject to two years' residence and payment of rates, with a number of fancy franchises for thrift, education, and other signs of a respectable status. Then when Gladstone and Bright transformed the bill, by amendments abolishing fancy franchises and introducing a lodger franchise, Disraeli accepted these changes one after another and gave the kingdom town household suffrage on a democratic basis. This he did with his eyes open, for he saw in an extended electorate the only hope of future power for a Conservative party that could not regain the leaders of ability who had left it with Peel. He managed the process so cleverly that though he lost two distinguished colleagues, Cranborne, the future Lord Salisbury, and Carnarvon, he carried the party with him. Cranborne called his conduct 'a political betrayal that has no parallel in our parliamentary annals', and said that the bill as it left the House of Commons was not Disraeli's but Gladstone's. In one sense this was true. If Gladstone and Bright had not pressed their amendments, the bill would have been a modest measure. On the other hand, Gladstone and Bright could never have induced the Lords to pass their bill. Disraeli's tactics in 1867 were much superior to Peel's in 1846. He did not take his party by surprise; he drew it gradually to the end he desired.

So Great Britain got household suffrage in the towns. Disraeli had no fears for the future of his party, and his confidence was justified by the history of the next half century; but he was disappointed by the immediate consequence, for the election of November 1868, in which he expected victory, gave the Liberals a majority estimated at 116. Mill said that when Disraeli (who had become Prime Minister in February 1868, when gout forced Derby to resign) told the new voters that he had given them the vote they replied : 'Thank you, Mr. Gladstone.' The reform debates of 1866–7 finally established Gladstone as the leader of a party in the country, though members of it in Parliament continued to distrust him. By sheer weight of personal and intellectual superiority, Gladstone forced himself on the Liberal party as its indispensable leader. Before and during the general election, in which he took an unusually active part, it was to him that the Liberal whips applied for advice; and with his approval they circulated—for the first time on a national scale—leaflets explaining party policy. Moreover, it was Gladstone who had the support in this new electorate. A contemporary observer remarked that he was 'the first official statesman who had convinced the working men that he really cared for them'. It was here that his power lay. In the House of Commons his 'transcendent abilities' brought him admiration, but not affection or confidence. It was the Liberals in the country and not the Liberals in Parliament who had played the part of Dido. A few years later, as we shall see, some of them were ready to complete the ominous passage from Dido's speech that Gladstone had quoted when he compared himself to the shipwrecked Aeneas. In the next six years he was to taste both triumph and tragedy.

Chapter Eight

Gladstone's First Government
(1868–74)

DISRAELI resigned as soon as the result of the general election was clear. Russell had intimated a year earlier that he would not take office again, and the Queen did not hesitate to summon Gladstone to become her Prime Minister. Nor did he hesitate to accept.

The situation was in one way like that in 1832. The sixties had been sterile, and the new Parliament found, like the first reformed Parliament, that a number of urgent problems demanded attention. Its lifetime was spent in the energetic treatment of those problems—in modernising our institutions, removing abuses, creating new machinery, meeting neglected needs, and giving vigour and body to administration, central and local. In some of these tasks it was brilliantly successful, so that Ensor the most judicial historian of this age could say of it that under many aspects it was the greatest administration during the long reign of Victoria. In others it failed, with grave consequences to the fortunes of the Liberal Party.

If sweeping reforms were overdue in England, much more were they overdue in Ireland. A simple contrast will show how the case stood between the two countries. There were many Acts on the Statute Book in 1870 to protect the British workman. There was not a single Act on the Statute Book to protect his counterpart the Irish peasant. On the other hand, there were several Acts to strengthen the powers of the landlord, and in the last forty years forty Coercion Bills had been passed. These facts reflected, not a virulent malignity on the part of Ireland's British rulers, but the influence of a fixed set of ideas which blinded them to the character of the Irish problem.

Nobody could hope to find a remedy for Irish misery and Irish discontent whose mind could not move outside this limited British orbit. It happened that two great British statesmen had shown at one time or another that they had this power. One was Disraeli. In 1844 he had summed up what he called 'the Irish question in its integrity' in a remarkable passage which was to be recalled to his attention later when he wished to forget it. 'What', he asked, 'was the duty of an English Minister? To effect by his policy all those changes which a Revolution would do by force.' By 1870 Disraeli had renounced these explosive opinions, and, after an attempt to reform the Irish land system in 1852 (which Derby thwarted), he had capitulated to the fashionable English view that if Ireland was in distress the fault was Irish rather than English.

The other Englishman who had been able to see the Irish problem in a larger light than his fellows was now Prime Minister. In 1845 Gladstone, travelling on the Continent and meeting important public men, was able to realise how the Irish problem looked to European minds, even to minds so friendly to England as Guizot.[1] The effect was seen in a passage in a

---

[1] He contemplated at one time visiting Ireland instead of France in 1845. Had he gone there, something not unlike the Naples letters might have been the result.

letter that he wrote at the time to his wife : 'Ireland, Ireland! That cloud in the West, that coming storm, the minister of God's retribution upon cruel and inveterate and but half-atoned injustice !' But Gladstone too had lapsed for a time into the errors of the 'enlightened' economists, and his extension of the income-tax to Ireland in 1853 showed, as he later admitted, that in his ardour as Chancellor of the Exchequer he had taken a superficial view of Ireland's claims. Before 1870 his earlier troubles of conscience had come back with full force. In 1867, when a series of Fenian outrages had caused great excitement, he had urged his countrymen not to forget the grievances of Ireland. When we had removed those grievances, he said in a very courageous speech, 'instead of hearing in every corner of Europe the most painful commentaries upon the policy of England towards Ireland—we may be able to look our fellow Europeans of every nation in the face'. It is not surprising that when warning of the Queen's summons reached him on 1 December 1868, he said : 'My mission is to pacify Ireland.'

In this spirit he passed two important Irish measures, in 1869 and 1870. The first disestablished the Irish Church, thereby removing a sensible Irish grievance. The second began the complex process of agrarian reform that was to occupy British statesmen for the next half-century. This Act started the social changes which gradually brought about the revolution that Disraeli had believed to be necessary in 1844.

To understand the problem it is necessary to trace in a summary manner the earlier history of Irish land and English conquest. The Irish land system was the result of a series of confiscations by which the soil of Ireland had passed into the ownership of immigrant conquerors. Until late in the eighteenth century, Catholics were forbidden to buy land or to take it on lease for more than thirty years. The landlords, as a rule, made no improvements and invested no capital. At the time of the Union a third of them were absentees, letting out their land to middlemen who sublet to peasants. Ireland had few industries, in consequence of hostile English legislation, and as its population grew rapidly, competition for farms became keen and landlords could get exorbitant rents. The tenants, large or small, had no security against eviction; on eviction they lost everything they had spent on improvements; and their landlords, unlike the landlords of England or Scotland, did not co-operate in improving anything. The labourers were in an even less enviable position; as Mill said, the Irish cottier, almost alone among mankind, could hardly be better off or worse off by any act of his own.

The fixed idea that had governed the British treatment of Ireland was that what Ireland needed was 'clearance'. The peasant was regarded as an anomaly. The famine of 1845-7, however terrible its fangs, had provided the remedy the economists had demanded. Over 700,000 people died of hunger and two millions emigrated. The 700,000 holdings under 15 acres were reduced to something not much over 300,000. At the same time a third of the landlords were ruined. Here was a great opportunity, and it was seized. Russell's Government passed an Encumbered Estates Act facilitating the sale of estates, and set up new courts which transferred much of the soil of Ireland to new owners.

The new landlords, mainly Irishmen with capital, meant to take money out of their estates. They cleared a good deal of the best land for grazing, and left the worst to the peasants. As good economists, they had little sentiment for their tenants, and the Government encouraged them to obey economic motives by passing two Acts to make eviction easier. In ten years families containing 200,000 people were turned out of their farms. If the British ideas that had been maintained so confidently for a century were sound, Ireland ought to have been on the road to comfort and contentment. Yet in 1868 Disraeli said that a fourth of the Irish people were helpless paupers, and in 1870 Gladstone said that the Irish labourers were as badly off as they had been in the eighteenth century under the Penal Laws.

Gladstone's Act of 1870 seems a modest reform in comparison with the bold revolution that he achieved in his second ministry. But it was an immense step forward. The best historian of the Irish agrarian problem, Pomfret, describes it as putting an end at one stroke to the two ideas that had dominated and guided British policy. The first was the virtue of *laisser faire*; the second the landlord's doctrine of an absolute and infallible right of property in land. Gladstone's measure recognised the tenant's retrospective right to compensation for improvements and his right to compensation for disturbance, thus substituting a law to protect the peasant for the legislation that had destroyed his rights and given power to the landlords.

There were serious deficiencies in the bill, as the Irish bishops (whom Gladstone consulted through Manning) saw at the time and as Gladstone discovered later. The bishops proposed to remove these deficiencies. That their criticism was well founded is apparent if we look ahead another ten years; for in 1881 Gladstone, who had thought he had settled the Irish agrarian problem, had to force through Parliament by his vast strength of character and intellect just the amendments that the bishops had proposed in 1870. (The need for them had become imperative as a result of the intervening revolution in European agriculture brought about by the development of the American prairies as grain-growing lands.) But no strength of character or intellect could have forced those amendments through Parliament in 1870. Nor would any Cabinet that could have been formed then have accepted them. Gladstone had to exhaust himself in a long struggle to persuade his colleagues to accept the revolutionary ideas of his bill of 1870 : revolutionary in implication if guarded in form. Morley described his Cabinet as 'in the main made up of landlords, lawyers, hardened and convicted economists,—not economists like Mill, but men saturated with English ideas of contract, of competitive rent, of strict rule of supply and demand'. With four of his colleagues—Clarendon, Argyll, Cardwell, and Lowe—Gladstone was in perpetual conflict. Bright was less helpful than he might have been, for he was full of his own ideas for land purchase. Those ideas found some scope in the bill, but Gladstone rightly pointed out that no scheme of land purchase could solve the problem of the great mass of the poor peasants, and that immediate protection was essential for men living at their landlords' mercy, liable to be thrown out on the hillside for no crime but poverty. The Acts of 1870 and of 1881 were necessary pre-

liminaries to any large scheme for transferring the soil
from the landlords to the peasants.

These reforms did not exhaust Gladstone's scheme
for the regeneration of Ireland, for atoning for past
injustice. He had two other plans in his head to bring
the government of Ireland into a more sympathetic
relation to the Irish people. For this purpose he
wanted, as Disraeli had wanted, to establish a Royal
Residence in Ireland, and he proposed to turn the
office of Viceroy into a purely ceremonial office. He
intended this post for the Prince of Wales. At the
same time he proposed to give Ireland a Minister who
would be a Secretary of State. These plans were foiled
by the Queen, who hated the idea of giving the
Prince of Wales any duties of importance, and feared
that she might be expected to visit Ireland more often
herself.

Gladstone's other effort also miscarried. In 1873 he
introduced a bill for Irish University Reform. He
worked with incessant vigour, reading, writing, thinking, and arguing, and produced a scheme for which
he made a brilliant defence in the House of Commons. Trinity College Dublin, Maynooth, and the
Colleges of Cork and Belfast were to be combined in
a single University. In the hope of reconciling the
opponents of mixed education, he excluded from the
curriculum theology, moral philosophy, and history.
The bill offended Catholics and Radicals alike
(though Manning supported it), and was defeated by
three votes, 43 Liberals voting in the majority. The
problem that Gladstone hoped to solve remained unsettled for another forty years, until Birrell solved it
in 1908 on different lines.

Gladstone had thus spent a good part of the energy

and time of his strong Government on his mission for pacifying Ireland. To understand what he accomplished and where he failed, two facts have to be remembered. The Irish Land Act proved a disappointment, partly because an amendment introduced by the Lords, which Gladstone had to accept, substituting 'exorbitant' for 'excessive' in the clause allowing a court to compensate a tenant dispossessed for non-payment of rent, was used by the landlords to check the operation of the Act. But the main reason for the failure of the Act was the agricultural slump of the late seventies. In 1875 a special correspondent of *The Times* visiting Ireland could report that 'at no period of her history did she appear more tranquil, more free from serious crime, more prosperous and contented'. Three years later there was universal distress and acute social war. Free trade, which had left agriculture uninjured at the time Disraeli denounced it, was now left with Disraeli as Premier to inflict irreparable damage on Irish economy. Even the English farming economy, though incomparably stronger, was broken up by the competition of wheat grown in the American Middle West far more cheaply than it could be grown in Europe. Ireland, as we shall see, was ruined.

Another phenomenon of the time was supremely important. The economists and politicians who had hailed the great exodus from Ireland as a welcome alleviation of their problems took a short-sighted view. The exodus carried the passions of Ireland across the Atlantic. The policy that dispeopled the Irish estates created a new Ireland overseas, nursing the fiercest resentments and the most implacable of hereditary hatreds. In 1867 Canada was invaded by the Fenians of the United States. That was a symptom of a new peril. Britain, finding Ireland a domestic anxiety, had turned her into an international danger. No man was to suffer more from the problems of this new warfare than the statesman who spent most of his life making atonement for the wrongs that had provoked it.

The policy of Gladstone's first government in foreign affairs, though it was called discreditable at the time, was in fact honourable both to the Prime Minister's sense of justice and to his sense of the possible. He took a keen and detailed interest in the work of the foreign service, and at all times of difficulty was in daily touch with his Foreign Secretary. This office was first entrusted to Clarendon, the man obviously fitted for it by abilities and by experience, who at once pressed on with negotiations already in hand for the settlement of the *Alabama* claims. A convention signed in January 1869 would have submitted the whole dispute to arbitration had it not been rejected by the American Senate as derogatory to the dignity of the Union. Gladstone and Clarendon did not entertain such exalted ideas of what was demanded by national honour. The Prime Minister set out their principles of foreign policy in a letter of 17 April 1869, to the Queen's secretary. They held, he said, that it was dangerous for England :

'to assume alone an advanced, & therefore an isolated position, in regard to European controversies; that come what may it is better for her to promise too little than too much : that she should not encourage the weak by giving expectations of aid, to resist the strong, but should rather seek to deter the strong, by firm but moderate language, from aggression on the weak; that she should seek to develop & mature the action of a common or public or European opinion, as the best standing bulwark against wrong . . .'

Such were the lines on which Gladstone conducted his foreign policies to the end; but it was not for long that he had the help of the sagacious Clarendon, the only professional diplomat ever to become Foreign Secretary and the only foreigner whose advice Napoleon III ever heeded. Clarendon devoted much effort, again with Gladstone's warm support, to an attempt in the winter of 1869–70 to persuade Prussia to join France in a scheme of disarmament. The old King of Prussia, like his grandson the last Kaiser, was obstinately sensitive in reacting against any suggestion that his armed forces should decrease, and his great Minister, Bismarck, had other activities in view for them. Nothing came of these talks.

On 27 June 1870, Clarendon died from overwork. Granville, his intimate colleague and a natural diplomat, Gladstone's closest political friend for the next two decades, succeeded him. Three weeks later France and Prussia were at war. Bismarck, wishing to draw attention away from his own share in its outbreak, used to say that more resolute action by England could have prevented the suddenly declared war, but this is certainly untrue. It is true that Granville, though a wise man, was not a quick one, and he lost time in elaborate consultations with Prime Minister and Cabinet before instructing Lyons in Paris to protest at the insensate precipitancy with which Napoleon's friends urged the Emperor to his doom; yet no English remonstrance, no matter how peremptory, would have held the French back from a war which they felt sure they would win, and in which the Prussians, equally certain of victory, were anxious to engage them.

Frenchman and Prussian alike thought his cause just, and denounced as hypocritical the attitude of a statesman who said he cared for justice and yet held back from a righteous war. But to Gladstone and Granville it was not clear which was the righteous side; wisely and responsibly, they thought it best to remain neutral. Granville entered at once into arrangements with both powers to secure the neutrality of Belgium also. This seemed to be threatened by a draft Franco-Prussian treaty of uncertain date published in *The Times* on 25 July. His new treaties were signed in the second week of August, in supplement to the guarantee of 1839 which they did not in any sense weaken.

September opened with the decisive German victory at Sedan and the fall of Napoleon's empire. France continued an almost hopeless resistance for five months more, but Bismarck was sure of victory, and on 22 September an offensive note from him delivered in London proclaimed the intention to secure Germany's western frontier by the annexation of Alsace and part of Lorraine, without consulting the 1,250,000 inhabitants concerned. Gladstone characterised this step as 'repulsive to the sense of modern civilization', and urged, first on Granville and then on his Cabinet, that this country ought to enter a formal protest in favour of the neutralising rather than the annexing of the disputed lands. After a sharp discussion in Cabinet, Granville defeated this proposal, on the grounds that it was ill timed and that Germany was in no mood to listen to reason. Goschen, a junior Minister, argued ably that it would be to the Liberal party's advantage to take up the cry of saving the Alsatians from oppression. This did not appeal to Gladstone, who continued later in the autumn to press his views on his colleagues in the interests not of party advantage but of international morality and of the future security of European peace. Through a private channel he also made an approach to Bismarck in February 1871; this was rebuffed. He could not persuade the Cabinet to agree with him, and in the end acquiesced in an annexation which he was powerless to prevent, the consequences of which, in Wilson's words, 'unsettled the peace of the world for nearly fifty years'.

During this period of office there was enough work to satisfy even Gladstone's gigantic appetite. During the session of 1871 he filled over 400 columns of Hansard; as his own Leader of the Commons, he hardly missed a sitting of the House, reporting lucidly on each to the Queen in the small hours before he went to bed; he was writing letters in his rapid hand at a rate equal to some six books of the present size in a year, letters that often called for powerful concentration of mind and an exact choice of words. He was still enough Peel's disciple to wish to know in detail what each of the great departments of State was doing, and always enough of a constitutionalist to submit every matter of the first importance to the judgment of his fifteen colleagues in Cabinet, and to defer to their opinion when he could not carry it with him. He felt deep responsibility, not unmixed with pleasure, in the making of Church appointments, to which he regularly devoted months of correspondence and hours of anxious thought.[1]

Though he was and is usually regarded as a weak judge of men, he had, nevertheless, assembled a Cabinet of unusual strength, hardly in need of the close attention which he devoted to all its members' doings. Gladstone did not find it possible at this stage to concentrate on a single issue at a time; heads of governments seldom can, for crises in politics seldom come singly. His attention was divided. Not only were there vital problems—Irish land, the Irish Church, peace with America, the reduction of jobbery,[2] the completion of the reform of 1867 by the introduction of compulsory schools and secret voting. There were also less crucial ones that needed his personal intervention for successful handling.

The most important of these issues was that of army reform. Edward Cardwell, a Peelite like his chief, spent the five years of this Government at the War Office, and at the cost of his own career (for the effort burnt him out) reorganised the British Army into a formidable fighting force. This task involved intricate and delicate negotiations with the Queen, which Gladstone had to undertake, to get her assent to the use of her prerogative to abolish the system by which officers bought promotion. This use, while entirely legal, did not make the Ministers who advised

[1] 'If you read in the papers some morning', he wrote to Bruce in February 1870, 'that I have been committed to Bedlam, & that a straight waistcoat is considered necessary, please to remember it will be entirely owing to the vacancy in the see of St. Asaph.'

[2] This was secured by insistence on examination for entry to the Civil Service. The foreign service was excluded from this reform: Gladstone may thus have obtained Clarendon's consent to the more important Irish Land Act.

it more popular either with the Conservative supporters of the old system, who thought truly enough that they had been tricked, or with the Radical wing of the Liberal party, which mistrusted royal prerogative on principle, at a moment when the Queen was at the height of her unpopularity. To Gladstone it seemed the proper and obvious way to assert the will of his constituted majority against the handful of officers who set the dangerous example of obstructing the passage of legislation on the subject through Parliament.[1]

A wider circle of opinion was antagonized in the winter of 1870–1, when Russia, acting in secret concert with Prussia, denounced the clause in the treaty that had ended the Crimean War which forbade her to keep a fleet in the Black Sea. This sudden repudiation caused Gladstone's Government an embarrassment that it took all his own intellectual agility and all Granville's diplomatic adroitness to allay. A conference early in 1871 assented to the principle that no treaty can be abrogated without the consent of all its signatories, and having thus secured the point of form went on at once to grant the point of substance in the Russian claim. To Gladstone who had disapproved the original restriction on Russia, the significant feature of the conference was its vindication of the rule of law in international affairs against mere force. To the strongly Russophobe British public what mattered was that Russia had got her way.

Gladstone and Granville proceeded to earn more unpopularity by another and even more important

---

[1] Gladstone himself is sometimes accused of having first exposed the possibilities of parliamentary obstruction in his prolonged struggle against the Divorce Act of 1857.

assertion of the rule of law. Negotiations over the *Alabama* claims were reopened, and in May 1871 both sides agreed to submit the dispute to arbitration. Some irresponsible Americans urged that Great Britain should be held to answer not only for all the *Alabama's* depredations, for the cost of hunting her down, and for the money her prey would have earned if unsunk, but even (with the help of a strained construction placed on British recognition of Southern belligerency) for almost the entire cost of the civil war to the North. Unofficial estimates of the damages due ran as high as the figure, considerable even today, of £400,000,000, twice the indemnity Prussia had just exacted from her beaten enemy. Gladstone kept his temper and kept his head amid the storms of American oratory, and held his colleagues, his subordinates, and his monarch to the need to recognise law and not force as the decisive factor. Eventually five arbitrators announced in September 1872 an award against Great Britain of three and a quarter million pounds, one-third of the figure to which the official American claims had been reduced. This was paid at once.[1]

This was regarded in the country as far too large a price to pay to end a dispute with a nation we did not fear. Some felt ashamed, and wondered that we no longer kept up the hectoring manners of Palmerston; others felt aggrieved, and complained that Gladstone's excessive subtlety had led him to agree to rules for the arbitration which were to the advantage of our opponent. In retrospect we can see that arbitration was a sensible way out of a difficulty that ought never

[1] Nearly a million pounds remain unclaimed, in the U.S. Treasury.

to have arisen. At the time it was taken for a sign that Gladstone was unfit to handle foreign affairs.

In home affairs he was hardly more popular. Forster's famous Education Act was passed in the summer of 1870, after prolonged debate, with the help of Conservative votes, because some Radical and Nonconformist Liberal M.P.s hoped for a measure that would have looked with less favour on Church of England schools; such a measure as Gladstone would certainly have opposed and no nineteenth-century House of Commons would have passed. Real benefit to Liberal principles followed the creation of a literate adult public, which made universal suffrage possible. Two years later Parliament passed another measure, the Ballot Act of 1872, securing to the newly enfranchised town workmen more benefit from the 1867 Reform Act than they had enjoyed in the particularly corrupt election of 1868. Though the ballot today seems a necessity, it was opposed at the time so strongly that the Ballot Act took up even more of the time of the Commons than the Education Act had done, was once rejected outright by the Lords, and antagonized from Government the opposite and conservative wing of the Liberals.

A third section of the Government's supporters was offended by Bruce's trade union legislation of 1871. Again great benefits, the legalisation of workmen's combinations and of strikes, were overlooked in anger at minor points—the declaration that picketing was illegal and the imposing of penalties on workmen who sought to impede their fellows from breaking a strike. It is curious that Gladstone should have paid no attention to the protests of working men against this plan, if ever he heard of their grounds for doing so, for these might have appealed to him. If strikes were to be legal, they said, then picketing ought to be legal also, since without it, in their view, strikes were impossible; and in the clauses prohibiting it no adequate definitions were given of what constituted obstruction, molestation, or intimidation.

Gladstone shared with many public men of his day some insensitiveness to the conditions of life of industrial workers, though in particular instances, as we have seen, this could be replaced by vigorous action on the workers' behalf. It seems strange that this man, who burned with indignation at the wrongs of the peoples of Bulgaria, Armenia, and Afghanistan, where he never set foot, who devoted the long evening of his life to the cause of Ireland which he visited once for three weeks, should have been stirred so little by the miseries of the people of England beside whom he lived. He had read enough of the classical economists to know how firmly they believed the engagement of workmen to be a contract between absolutely unfettered individuals, yet was not himself economist enough to feel competent to challenge them on their own ground. His attitude here can be compared with that of the staunch Radical, Bright, to Shaftesbury's Ten Hours' Act: Bright was so impressed with the economists' arguments that he voted against it. On this particular issue of trade unionists' rights, Gladstone did not find himself aware of a manifest injustice calling to be righted; only such awareness inspired his great campaigns.

Gladstone may well have agreed with Bruce that the matter of picketing was not important enough to demand his attention by comparison with the struggle to secure the ballot and the delicate negotiation with

America, both of which were in progress at the time. His conduct of politics under the pressure of work which he imposed on himself suffered in skill and acuteness as time went on. The last three years of his first Cabinet were productive of fewer results and more friction than the first two had been. In March 1873, on being narrowly defeated on Irish universities, he seized the occasion to resign. Disraeli instantly refused to take office. For a week he and Gladstone carried on a somewhat ludicrous exchange of letters through the Queen, each unwilling to accept the responsibility either of governing the country or of advising a dissolution, and in the end Gladstone's Cabinet resumed their tasks, shaken in nerve and reputation.

Their last ten months in office were unhappy, particularly so for their leader. A minor scandal at the Post Office compelled several Cabinet changes, as a result of which Gladstone foolishly resumed his old task as Chancellor of the Exchequer as well as all his other duties. In the drab intoxication of Treasury figures and in petty plans for saving money, he lost his grip on the grand problems of politics, embarked on a grandiose but chimerical project for abolishing income tax, and dissolved Parliament impulsively early in 1874.[1] He expected victory at the polls, but the Conservatives gained a majority of at least 48.

[1] A curious complication about his own seat in the Commons has often, though wrongly, been held responsible for this dissolution. In the general election of 1868, though his party was triumphant, he himself just failed to win the seat which he contested in South-west Lancashire (somewhat altered from the seat which he had won by 300 odd votes in South Lancashire when Oxford rejected him in 1865). This, as some of his friends reminded him, was like the warning of mortality that a slave used to whisper in the ear of a

Several reasons can be given for this. In the first place, the ballot had a result unforeseen by anyone in London : it created an Irish party not bound to either of the English parties, which returned 58 members of whom we shall hear more, a majority for their country pledged to pursue its nationalist aims. Secondly, the Liberal Government was discredited by bickerings among its leaders at home and by an inglorious foreign record. Thirdly, some of its more extreme supporters were so distressed by its measures for education and against picketing that they stayed away from the polls. Moreover, many voters were persuaded to vote Conservative by the publicans, who were enraged at a licensing Act passed by Bruce in 1872 which (as Ensor pointed out) established the permanent alliance between Conservatism and the liquor trade. Gladstone thought this critical, and wrote to his brother : 'We have been borne down in a torrent of gin and beer.'

Above all, Disraeli had not wasted his five years in opposition. He had set up the first efficient centralised English party organization, on lines that survive to this day. It had won him seats steadily at by-

Roman General as he rode through the city in triumph. Gladstone had already been elected, without visiting the constituency or requesting the honour, for Greenwich, and it was doubted by his Whips whether he could hold Greenwich in a by-election, though in a general election his chances were (correctly, as it turned out) thought good. It was uncertain as the law then stood whether his assumption of the office of Chancellor of the Exchequer as well as First Lord of the Treasury necessitated his resignation and a new contest for his Greenwich seat. Some have thought that he dissolved Parliament in order to secure his own return without such a by-election. In fact, the best legal advice given to him was that there was no need for a by-election, and he asked the Queen for a dissolution not from personal but from general political motives.

elections in the previous autumn, and it had candidates ready in every constituency which he could conceivably hope to win. The general election of 1874 was the first triumph of the Conservative Central Office, and it made Disraeli Prime Minister for the second time. He, however, was already in his seventieth year, and felt that real power had come 'too late'.

Chapter Nine

Bulgarian Horrors
(1875–9)

GLADSTONE resigned office before Parliament met, and explained in a published letter to Granville that he meant to take a long holiday (he had had none while Prime Minister). A year later he formally resigned, as he had long intended to do, the leadership of the Liberal party, and indicated that he proposed gradually to withdraw from political life altogether. His various projects to retire have been much controverted, then and since. This first intention to withdraw must be accepted as sincere by anyone who considers the evidence for it in Gladstone's papers, unless he is convinced that Gladstone's whole life in politics was hypocrisy and sham. At the time of the election, the Prime Minister was sixty-four; he remembered that Canning had died at fifty-seven, Herbert at fifty, Peel at sixty-two; he knew that he had deserved well of his country, though for the time its verdict had gone against him. The concern with religion which had always been strong in him became dominant, and in his own phrase he 'deeply desired an interval between parliament and the grave'. So he withdrew to Hawarden.

Yet habits of controversy which went back to his earliest boyhood could not be laid aside.[1] An article

[1] A decade later this was easier; see p. 169 below.

of his in October 1874 included a savage by-blow at the Church of Rome ('no one can become her convert without renouncing his moral and mental freedom, and placing his civil loyalty and duty at the mercy of another . . . she has equally repudiated modern thought and ancient history'). To deal with the scores of protests he received, he published next month a brief 'Political Expostulation', which attacked the decree of papal infallibility pronounced four years before, on the ground that it weakened to the point of destruction the loyalty of Catholics to their various temporal rulers. Nearly 150,000 copies were sold at once, and for a few months the resulting controversy was intense. The points in dispute are tedious today; but the incident illustrates Gladstone's political honesty. To write a strongly anti-Roman popular pamphlet was no way to ingratiate his party with the Roman Catholic people of Ireland, whose members of Parliament might later be needed to support it. Yet Gladstone believed, not without vehemence, that he was right, and therefore had to speak out.

He paid too little attention to his party while he was not its leader. Hartington, who succeeded him as its chief in the Commons (Forster being even less acceptable to the Radicals), found himself embarrassed more than once by Gladstone's unheralded interventions in the House or in the country. It seems today as if Gladstone could not have failed to notice the inconvenience that he caused, but today's historians cannot help regarding the nineteenth century with the eyes of the twentieth. Party discipline was not important to a man brought up in a Canningite household, who had come of age in 1830, who remembered the brilliance of Lowe's quite recent speeches on reform that had flouted party and brought down a government in the interest of what that wayward orator thought right. In 1875 Gladstone enjoyed the presidency of the Metaphysical Society and busied himself with articles on Homer and religion. In the summer of the following year he was working on an article on 'Future Retribution': his notes bear the docket: 'From this I was called away to write on Bulgaria.'

The call was as compelling as had been the call a generation earlier to expose the horrors of the Neapolitan prisons. In 1876 the whole of the Balkan peninsula, except for the Dalmatian coast and for Greece south of Thessaly, was still under the suzerainty of Turkey; but as Gladstone well knew, for his range of European acquaintance included several Balkan notables, the Christian peoples of the peninsula were achieving a national consciousness and growing restive at control from Constantinople. In the summer of 1875 there were revolts in Bosnia, which spread next year to Bulgaria; in the latter territory Anatolian troops suppressed the insurgents with a brutality that considered neither age nor sex. A *Daily News* reporter sent home in June and July 1876 dispatches that described a cruel and anarchical society in which a Christian child could not scamper through its home village without danger to its life. Inquiries by the British and American consuls on the spot, while they did not confirm all the reporter's stories, made it plain that well over ten thousand Bulgarians had been put to death, often by torture, without trial.

Disraeli, whose failing health compelled him this autumn to retire to the House of Lords as Earl of

Beaconsfield, did not at first treat these stories seriously, and Gladstone felt himself compelled to rouse the feelings of Englishmen against the atrocities of Ottoman rule. He published in September *The Bulgarian Horrors and the Question of the East,* a pamphlet of which forty thousand copies were sold within four days. He contended that the statesmen of the Christian powers ought as Christians, and indeed as men, to protest at the outrages of the Turk; and that those powers ought to act in concert for a great Christian object, to deprive Turkey of control over her Balkan provinces. Moreover, as he put it in a speech at Blackheath on 9 September, 'if anyone asked me how I would distribute the spoils, my answer would be this—I would not distribute them at all. These provinces were not destined to be the property of Russia, or of Austria, or of England; they were destined for the inhabitants of the provinces themselves'. This doctrine of self-determination for small national groups was fundamental in Gladstone's foreign policy, and twenty years after his death it was accepted as the grand principle on which Europe was to be divided up by the peace settlement of 1919–20. It was not new when he brought it forward in 1876, for it had inspired both Canning and Palmerston, but it was bitterly and at first effectively controverted in Beaconsfield's England.

'Indignation is froth, except as it leads to action', said Gladstone in his first pamphlet. To his distress, his indignation did not at first lead to any substantial movement of opinion in the country, and in May 1877 he was defeated on the issue in Parliament by 354 to 223. By this time the growing complications of the European crisis were beginning to favour his opponents. Serbia, autonomous but not independent, declared war on Turkey and was defeated; in April 1877 Russia declared war on Turkey in her turn, to avenge the Serbs, and ten months later succeeded in compelling a Turkish surrender. Russia forced on Turkey peace terms that included a huge Bulgaria, but in so doing contravened so many provisions of the treaties of 1856 and 1871 that, bearing in mind the terms of the latter, she had to agree to submit the whole question to a Congress of the Powers, which met at Berlin in midsummer 1878.

Disraeli meanwhile had been conducting what Palmerston would have approved as a 'spirited foreign policy'. With a skill equalled by his audacity, he brought Great Britain right up to the brink of war with Russia without ever letting a shot be fired from a British gun, succeeded in impressing the Russians with his determination to fight if they did not withdraw from some at least of their pretensions, and agreed with them privately before the Congress met what decisions should be reached at it. He went to Berlin himself, enjoyed the pomp and circumstance, impressed even Bismarck with his masterly qualities as a diplomat, and returned to England in July 1878 to proclaim 'Peace with Honour'. He played with supreme adroitness on the Russophobe proclivities of the London public, and Dilke recorded in March 'the ordinary Sunday afternoon diversion of the London rough' as 'going to howl at Mr. Gladstone' in his house in Harley Street. But his efforts exhausted Disraeli so far that he was unable to take advantage of the tide of opinion when it was setting in his favour just after the Congress ended, and a general election was postponed.

This gave Gladstone a chance from which boos and broken windows could not divert him. He set out to work up opinion against Beaconsfield and what he called Beaconsfieldism, first through the normal channel of articles in the monthly reviews, then by a new political departure. Government policy helped him, for during 1879 Disraeli's distant lieutenants pursued courses in South Africa and on the North-West Frontier of India which brought on expensive little wars, and British defeats at the hands both of Zulus and of Pathans who could not convincingly be portrayed as aggressors.

In November 1879, ignoring the offer of a safe seat in Leeds, he set out to canvass Midlothian, the metropolitan constituency of Scotland, where (at the young Rosebery's suggestion) he put himself forward as a parliamentary candidate against Dalkeith, the son of his own old colleague in Peel's Cabinet, one of the greatest magnates in Scotland, the Duke of Buccleuch. Up to this time speeches in the country had only been made, as a rule, by sitting members during parliamentary recesses, and were little regarded by public opinion or the Press. Cobden and Bright, in their attack on the Corn Laws in the forties, had provided the main exception. In a fortnight's work Gladstone ended this system for good, and revolutionised the political situation by a series of addresses to the Scottish electors whose votes he would seek whenever the dissolution came. Every word that he spoke was reported all over the kingdom next day, by a Press that had not yet devoted its energies to non-political fields; the effect outside Midlothian was large, and within it electrical. He needed to be heard and seen to secure his full effect.

He was able to strike home to his hearers, through the famous eye, the controlled gestures, and the urgent tones of the deep voice, the idea that each of them personally was answerable for the wrongs done to the Balkan Christians, and that each of them personally was able by casting his vote aright to make amends for disaster and to build a better and more Christian Europe.

There was much for Gladstone to attack. He thought Northcote's finance unsound, and said so at length and with a wealth of detail; he regarded some of Disraeli's actions as unconstitutional, for the latter had moved Indian troops to the Mediterranean without the consent of Parliament and had concluded secret arrangements both with Turkey and with Russia—his Anglo-Turkish convention made Cyprus a British colony—without assuring himself that they would be welcomed either by parliamentary or by public opinion; above all, Gladstone disapproved the 'forward' policies of Disraeli's agents in South Africa and Afghanistan. These gave rise to two famous sentences in one of the Midlothian speeches, that sum up his whole appeal as a man to other men : 'Remember the rights of the savage, as we call him. Remember that the happiness of his humble home, remember that the sanctity of life in the hill villages of Afghanistan among the winter snows, is as inviolable in the eye of Almighty God as can be your own.'

When last the Eastern Question had been before the attention of the British public, at the time of the Crimean War, Palmerston had attuned himself to the bellicose mood of the electorate, and his few well-intentioned opponents, Cobden, Gladstone, and Bright at their head, had been derided in the country; Cobden and Bright had lost their seats in the election that followed the war. In 1879 Gladstone succeeded where in 1855 Cobden and Bright had failed. He swung public opinion round into opposition to the Palmerstonian foreign policy of Disraeli, and in doing so he justified his own faith in the widening of the electorate. When the general election finally took place in March and April 1880 there were contests in an unusually large number—over three-quarters—of the seats, and the Liberals won a success as great as that of their opponents six years before. Their majority over Conservatives and Irish combined was at least 46, and Gladstone was returned with an adequate majority for Midlothian.

To some extent the Liberals' victory was due to the application of lessons learned from their Conservative opponents. The Radical Lord Mayor of Birmingham, Joseph Chamberlain, who will appear in these pages again, had already organized a National Liberal Federation, copied from the Conservative Central Office and American party 'machines', that was efficient enough to carry 60 of the 67 seats it contested, and to that extent—one-sixth of the Liberal seats— the victory was not Gladstone's own, for many Radicals, such as Chamberlain and Dilke, looked on his campaign with suspicion. The arch-enemy for them was Russia, and they mistook enmity to Russia's opponents for friendship with that country, whose despotism they could not forgive. In fact, Gladstone was not then or ever unduly pro-Russian; he simply admitted the fact that Russian policy in the Balkans had much more to justify it than had the policy of Constantinople.

The other wing of the Liberal party was hardly

less reluctant to follow Gladstone on his Balkan adventure. To the cautious and sober Whigs the campaigns in Midlothian seemed demagogic and distasteful, and were not in harmony with the established principle that foreign policy is a matter on which wide discretion must be left to the Government of the day. Even Granville found himself at loggerheads with Gladstone more than once, and Hartington made no secret of his divergence. When on 21 April Disraeli resigned, the attitude of these two noblemen was important, for Queen Victoria sent for them and asked them to form a Government. This was a perfectly proper step for her to take, though she did not conceal from either of them the strong antipathy which she had by now conceived for Gladstone, nor how marked was her reluctance to enter into official relations with him again. However, neither Granville nor Hartington dared to form a Ministry to which Gladstone did not belong, and the latter, while polite and courteous as always, made it clear that he would not serve in anybody else's Government. There was no doubt that opinion in the country looked to him as the head of the next Cabinet, and the Queen bowed to necessity. On 23 April 1880, Gladstone for the second time kissed hands as Prime Minister.

Chapter Ten

Ireland Again
(1880–2)

ALTHOUGH Gladstone was felt at court to have forced himself into power by Radical means, half of the Cabinet which he formed was composed of noblemen and only two of his colleagues in it were Radicals: the Radicalism of one of these, Bright, was much dimmed with time. The other, Joseph Chamberlain, the most energetic figure in the new Government, was forced on the Prime Minister much against the latter's will. Gladstone neither liked nor understood this violent man, whose political abilities were second only to his own, who came from a different social class, whose very religion was strange (in Gladstone's eyes) to the point of heresy, and who had brought himself before public attention through the channel of local government in which Gladstone had seldom taken interest. The Government, which seemed in the phrase of today to have received so decisive a mandate from the electorate, was divided against itself throughout its five years of life.

Its majority in the Commons was no more homogeneous, though it seemed large: 347 Liberals against 240 Conservatives, and 65 Irish Nationalists, was one authoritative estimate at the time. In the election the Liberals had a decisive majority of the votes cast. Many of them, however, were cast in two-member constituencies, in which the two successful candidates had often been chosen to appeal to different strata of the electorate. Party boundaries had not yet set fast, and many nominal Liberals had still much that was Conservative in them, nor was party discipline so rigid as to ensure that members would vote as their party leaders rather than their own consciences, or their own interests, dictated. Brand, the Speaker, remarked at once that the Liberals in the Commons were 'not only strong, but determined to have their own way in spite of Mr. Gladstone'.

An immediate difficulty arose when the new Parliament met at the end of April. Charles Bradlaugh, one of the Liberal members for Northampton, was an aggressive atheist, and was refused permission by the Commons either to affirm or to take the oath of allegiance. A wretched controversy on this issue was dragged out all through the next five years. The Conservative opposition sought to ally Bradlaugh's defenders with Bradlaugh's beliefs, which notoriously extended to the advocacy of birth control as well as the denial of God. Gladstone detested Bradlaugh's opinions, but realised that they were not the most important matter at issue. No one who called himself a Liberal or cared for liberty, he thought, could possibly take it on himself to say that the holding of particular opinions, however reprehensible in themselves, ought to put a man outside the pale of the legislating class; moreover, no one who cared for democracy could ignore the steadfast desire of the electors of Northampton to be represented by Bradlaugh, whom they continued to return at a series of by-elections. So Gladstone defended Bradlaugh's claim to sit in the House in some of the most magnificent of all his speeches, but not even his oratory could persuade a majority of the Commons to his view.

He found himself opposed by a much younger man of almost equal brilliance as a speaker, Lord Randolph Churchill, who was only thirty-one when Parliament met. With the help of two or three friends Churchill set out to instil vigour into an opposition which he found excessively staid under the leadership of Northcote, who was twice his own age and had never lost the respect for Gladstone acquired when he had been the latter's private secretary at the Board of Trade. Churchill's little group, nicknamed the 'Fourth Party', found in the Bradlaugh case both a stick with which to beat the Government and a ladder by which to climb to notoriety. Its leader was conspicuous throughout the dispute, which was not settled until after the next general election, when a new Speaker (Peel's son) allowed Bradlaugh to take the oath and his seat and forbade the House to question his decision.[1]

This disagreeable incident provided one of the most tiresome of the Prime Minister's preoccupations. His original intention on taking power had been to bring the Eastern question to a satisfactory conclusion at once, and then to retire. He and Granville, again Foreign Secretary, achieved a settlement here with unexpected ease, but a remorseless pressure of events compelled Gladstone to remain for five years in an office which he hated, and hated more and more as time went on, to deal with a succession of difficulties

[1] The House of Commons eventually repented and in 1891 when Bradlaugh was on his deathbed ordered the most savage of the resolutions passed against him to be deleted from its journals.

hardly any of which he had foreseen, and in the end to resign with diminished reputation and with tasks now cherished still unperformed.

The foreign problem was to convince the Sultan of Turkey that he had got to carry out the cessions of territory laid down by the Treaty of Berlin, and that he could no longer rely on British support in evading the loss. Goschen, as special ambassador to Constantinople, managed eventually to secure the cession of Dulcigno to Montenegro in the autumn of 1880 and of all Thessaly to Greece in the spring of 1881. This was the biggest change of a European frontier secured without a war in the nineteenth century, but it can hardly be claimed as a triumph for Gladstonian principles of international politics, since the Sultan only surrendered to a direct threat of force applied Palmerston-fashion by our Mediterranean fleet. Granville put the position compactly in a note to his wife of October 1880 : 'Present failure, extreme difficulties in every alternative, and only chance of real success resting upon rather a gambling *coup*.' The gamble succeeded, but through British power alone, not from the Concert of Europe that Gladstone wished to further and in terms of which he always contemplated European affairs. Moreover, though he withdrew from Asia Minor the 'military consuls' with whom Disraeli had begun to penetrate it, he was not able to repudiate Disraeli's Cyprus Convention and hand that island over to Greece. The Queen disapproved repudiation strongly, and Granville warned him that British opinion would hardly be more favourable; there were more pressing claims on Gladstone's time, and the question of Cyprus was put on one side.

In forming his Cabinet he made a needless diversion of his own energies into unimportant channels when he saw fit to take over once again the work of Chancellor of the Exchequer. He had an alternative Chancellor available in Childers, to whom he eventually surrendered the post at the end of 1882, calling him indeed 'a much better finance minister than myself'. By that time he had spent nearly three years in toiling at the financial details which exercised so compelling a fascination over a mind that was capable of ranging over wider and more fruitful fields. The financial machine established by his own earlier efforts performed its work so efficiently that its care should have been left to a subordinate, for there was an Imperial crisis of the first importance that demanded all Gladstone's attention.

During his years in opposition after 1874, the relations between England and Ireland had been transformed. Disraeli had been concerned with dreams of Empire so wide that some of his critics have suspected them of being altogether removed from actuality, and he had forgotten the terse analysis of Ireland's wrongs which he had delivered in 1844. He did nothing for Ireland. He never went to Ireland; even Gladstone, who spent a generation at work on its problems, visited it once only, for three weeks spent in country houses in 1877, which can have taught him nothing of what he should have gone to see. Buckle wisely remarked in his *Life of Disraeli* that 'these facts must seem incredible, were they not true.'

Disraeli's Government opened its career with some useful Acts, consolidating the work of its predecessor, to improve the conditions of the workmen in England's new industrial towns. But because Disraeli did nothing for Ireland, Irishmen therefore made it impossible for him to do anything for England either during his last three years in power. These Irishmen were members of Parliament elected, thanks to the Ballot Act of 1872, in entire independence of the Anglo-Irish landlords, who had hitherto ensured that their tenantry voted for whichever of the two English parties they supported themselves. They found a movement for Irish Home Rule already in being, under the decorous management of Isaac Butt, a kindly and agreeable Dublin lawyer. Butt they elbowed out of the way, for kindliness brought no results; they forced English attention to Irish grievances by making it almost impossible for the House of Commons to transact business on any other domestic subject.

The House's rules of debate had been drawn up gradually over many decades, and were designed to give private members the fullest opportunities to question executive action; since before Cabinet government of the modern type was established the House regarded itself (as the United States Congress still regards itself) as a necessary check on the executive. Up to this time these opportunities had never been exploited to the full, and members who had now and again made use of them—Gladstone in the 1857 divorce debates, 'the Colonels' in the army debates of 1870—were felt to be taking unfair advantage of other honourable members who were honest even if possibly mistaken. Honesty was a quality that the new Irish M.P.s did not attribute to their English opponents, and they ensured that the House wasted the greater part of the time that it spent in session.

Dilatory motions of every kind were moved, and the troubles of Ireland were brought to bear on the subject-matter of almost every debate. That the triumphs of Disraeli's last years in office after 1876 are to be sought abroad and not at home is a mark of the difficulty that faced his party in any attempt to legislate on home affairs.

A young Anglo-Irish Protestant squire, whose arrival to take his seat in 1875 happened to coincide with an early attempt at obstructing the work of the Commons, soon imposed himself on the Irish nationalist party as its leader. Charles Stewart Parnell belonged to the Irish squirearchy on his father's side; his American mother taught him to detest the English ruling class. Hesitant and unconvincing as a public speaker, proud and reserved in private conversation, he yet was able to assert himself by force of character as a man to be obeyed. He treated all Englishmen with remote aloofness, and they reciprocated his distaste. He was hardly more affable to his Irish followers, but these recognised in him a force that could do something for Ireland, and did as he bade them.

A parallel movement in Ireland was even more important than the obstruction engineered by Parnell at Westminster. Michael Davitt, its organising genius, had nothing in common with Parnell but the year of his birth (1846). The child of peasants, evicted on to the hillside with his family when he was five, he had moved as a labouring child to Lancashire and lost an arm in an accident at work when he was eleven. Not unnaturally the Fenian revolutionary movement attracted him, and in 1870 he was sentenced to fifteen years' hard labour for collecting arms. While in prison, he decided that an economic rather than a political solution was the only possible one for Ireland's wrongs. On being released [1] in 1877, he set about the founding of an Irish Land League, which he achieved two years later with Parnell's help. The object of the League was to mitigate the catastrophe which fell on Irish agriculture at the end of the seventies, by reducing exorbitant rents and by enabling tenants to buy their holdings outright. Davitt intended the League to act by pressure of public opinion on landlords, exercised through mass meetings in the country towns, and that, indeed, was the form that its agitation took and to which its leaders tried to confine it. But conditions in the Irish countryside were too bad, the peasantry too destitute, the sense of oppression too strong. Young men who heard the League's speakers denounce rack-renting succumbed easily to the temptation to maim the rack-renter's cattle, or to snipe at his agent in a country lane. As the tale of evictions mounted in Ireland, so did the tale of outrages.

This was the situation with which Gladstone had to deal on becoming Prime Minister in 1880. As a temporary measure, he sought to pass a bill to compensate tenants who were evicted because the last two harvests were so bad that they could not pay their rents. He recognised, as he wrote to Argyll, that in the current Irish crisis, with the people at the point of starvation, 'it is impossible to apply without qualification of any kind the ordinary rules of property'. The amendment which the Lords had insisted on introducing into his Land Act of a decade before prevented that Act from having the effect for which

[1] On ticket-of-leave. He was twice subsequently imprisoned again.

Gladstone had hoped, and landlord spirit in the Upper House was still strong. His compensation bill was defeated there by 282 to 51 on 3 August 1880.

There was nothing for it then but to prepare another Land Act, this time one that would cut nearer to the root of the matter. With characteristic energy, subtlety, and single-mindedness, Gladstone engaged in this task in the winter of 1880–1. Conservative as he had always been of established institutions, he sought at first to keep his former Act in sight, but detailed study of the problem convinced him that a mere expansion of the old measure would not satisfy present needs. He did not range far enough in preparation, for he failed to consult either Parnell, who understood the problem from the Irish point of view, or Chamberlain, with whom he was never in sympathy. Yet he ranged very far. He presented at last a bill of such astonishing complexity that it was said that no one but himself and Thring, the Treasury counsel who helped him draft it, really understood it all. This much at least was clear, that under the bill the tenants of all Ireland would enjoy rents agreed by new rent courts to be fair, security against arbitrary eviction, and a right to sell their tenancy to anyone of whom the landlord did not disapprove. It was not an easy bill to drive through a Whiggish Cabinet, a Commons lukewarm at best, and a hostile House of Lords. So few of his colleagues had their hearts in the measure that Gladstone had to undertake personally its defence in 58 sittings of the Lower House; eventually the bill became law. With its passing began the necessary Irish agricultural revolution, for its operation reduced rents enough to make possible at last, through the purchase by farmers of the plots they tilled, the creation of the landowning peasantry in which Irish agriculture has found its eventual salvation.

Unfortunately the land question was not the only side of Irish discontent that needed treatment. The problem of public order was equally acute and to Gladstone even more distressing. His Government began by allowing their predecessors' Coercion Act to lapse; but the tale of murder and outrage grew worse. The spur to outrage was, in fact, not coercion but eviction, and the Lords' rejection of the Compensation for Disturbance Bill, by preventing a brake on eviction, prevented also a brake on outrages, news of which continued to lower the English opinion of the Irish and reduce the chances of any settlement. From this closed circle of misunderstanding and distress Gladstone sought to find a way out with his Land Act, and the only way in which he could make the Act palatable to Parliament was in passing first a Coercion Act of a peculiarly severe kind. Forster, the Irish Secretary, was given by this Act powers of arbitrary arrest hardly less extensive than Bomba's. In opposing this measure the Irish members once kept the Commons in session for forty-one hours at a stretch, until the Speaker on his own initiative closed the sitting; to ensure the continuance of any parliamentary government at all, Gladstone had to supervise the introduction of the first arrangements for the closure of debate, since greatly extended.

He hated to make these plans, which clashed with his essentially conservative Liberalism; he hated coercion still more, for it clashed with his instinct for freedom. Yet he thought coercion the necessary price for a land reform without which Ireland would have to remain miserable, and he paid it in the bitter first two months of 1881, before he embarked on the four-month struggle to secure the Land Act. Until the Land Act was passed evictions could go on, and so long as evictions went on, outrages in answer to them continued, in spite of the increased powers of Forster's police. The odious work of repression wore down Forster's energy and warped his judgement—not the only judgement to go awry in the summer and autumn of 1881. The Land League's leaders, while they recognised that the Land Act brought genuine benefits to the peasants, thought that it was a concession extracted from a hostile Government by force, and proceeded to apply more force in order to extract more concessions.

Parnell and Gladstone, at cross purposes, made public speeches during the recess that revealed their distrust of each other. Gladstone had been working secretly, and in vain, to persuade his Cabinet colleagues to allow Ireland a larger measure of self-government. They pressed him instead to denounce Parnell and the League. When he concluded a speech at Leeds with the remark that 'the resources of civilisation are not yet exhausted', intended to throw Parnell on his guard, the latter defied him, calling him at Wexford 'this masquerading knight-errant, this pretending champion of the rights of every other nation except those of the Irish nation'. The Cabinet met to consider Parnell's attitude, and rashly agreed to his arrest (despite his membership of Parliament) under the Coercion Act. On 13 October Parnell found himself in Kilmainham jail.

Parnell, who unlike Davitt was well treated in prison, appeared a martyr to the Irish, and with his moderating hand removed, the atrocities of 'Captain Moonlight' grew ever blacker. There were fourteen murders and sixty-one attempted murders in the Irish countryside in the six months that followed Parnell's arrest. The Land League was not violent enough for the Irish extremists, who formed secret societies with revolutionary aims. By April 1882 Parnell was anxious to leave prison so that he might try to reassert himself over the various anti-British movements that seemed to bring Ireland nightly nearer anarchy. He let it be known to Gladstone that he was now prepared to support the operation of the Land Act instead of denouncing it as hypocritical; he was at once released. There was an understanding between him and the Cabinet that a bill would be introduced at Westminster to deal with the tenants whose rents were in arrears—this Parnell rightly regarded as necessary to the sound working of the Land Act. In return, Parnell was to do what he could to modify the violence of the Irish land agitators.

This understanding was negotiated by Parnell with Chamberlain, who put himself forward as spokesman for the Cabinet, through two channels: the reliable Justin McCarthy and the vain Captain O'Shea, the husband of Parnell's mistress. The use of the second channel had unfortunate results, for O'Shea gave Forster a copy of a letter from Parnell, written to keep O'Shea quiet, of which Forster made damaging use in the Commons soon afterwards. Party bickering at Westminster was so intense in this decade that the unintended suggestion in this letter of a disreputable deal behind the scenes between Government and the nationalist leader was eagerly seized on and exploited by the enemies of both. Forster was in a fit of bad political temper. He resigned his office on the day (2 May) that his colleagues decided on Parnell's release, not only because he alone disagreed with their decision, but also, it seems probable, because he was worn out with the cares of Dublin and anxious to get away.

For a moment it seemed as though an answer to the Irish question was in sight. Parnell began at once to exercise such influence as he could to moderate agrarian excess; and Gladstone sent over to Ireland his old friend Spencer (Althorp's nephew) as Viceroy, with a seat in Cabinet and general responsibility under himself for Irish policy. To succeed Forster Gladstone chose Hartington's brother, Lord Frederick Cavendish. Gladstone knew him well, not only because he had married Mrs. Gladstone's niece, but also because he had been for the past two years Gladstone's principal subordinate at the Treasury. This admirable man crossed to Dublin on 5 May. Next evening he and Burke, the permanent head of the Irish executive, were both stabbed to death in broad daylight, almost under the eyes of the Viceroy, in Phœnix Park.

The murders were found long afterwards to have been the work of a secret society which had been trying for some weeks to kill Forster, had picked on Burke as a substitute, and had killed Cavendish without knowing who he was. They put an end to any chance of an immediate Irish settlement. Everyone felt that an even harsher Coercion Act had to be passed; this did, towards the end of the year, begin to have an appreciable effect in putting down crime, for under it magistrates could hold secret inquiries without formulating a charge against anyone. (It was in this way that the treachery of two members of the society revealed the 'Invincibles', the murderers of Cavendish and Burke.) Moreover, Gladstone held to his arrangement of April with Parnell, who had been seriously alarmed by the killings in Phœnix Park, and persuaded Parliament to pass an Arrears Act which made the Land Act of 1881 workable. So the economic position of the Irish peasant gradually improved, though distrust and hatred continued to keep Irishmen and Englishmen apart. One incident will show how this mistrust could be kept in being through events themselves apparently outside politics. On 17 August 1882, a group of Irishmen on the mountain of Maamtrasna in Connemara broke into a neighbour's cabin to murder him, his wife, and their four children. One of the sons survived; other neighbours had watched the murderers approach the hut, and informed against them. In the end, eight of them were condemned to death, of whom three were hanged. None of them, or of the witnesses, spoke any language but Erse. The tale brought forcibly before the English the desolate misery and brutality of the Irish countryside, and before the Irish the cruel unreliability of English justice. There were grave doubts about whether one of the hanged men, Myles Joyce, had really been guilty, or had been the victim of senseless police spite. This made a petty tribal quarrel into a great political issue, for once doubts were cast on the impartiality of English justice, English government was visibly crumbling at its foundations. Dilke, taking a long walk near Dublin with Spencer, found him 'assailed by the majority of those we met with shouts of, "Who killed Myles Joyce?"' In the end Spencer, on mature consideration, decided that justice had run its proper course, and his Conservative successor, who also looked into the case carefully, agreed with him. Yet Irish suspicion remained.

G. O. Trevelyan, the new Irish Secretary, was a Radical, but without the force of Chamberlain, who should perhaps have had the appointment. Yet to appoint Chamberlain would have meant for Gladstone both throwing over Spencer and surrendering into younger hands the control of the Irish affairs that he felt no British statesman but himself had fully understood.

It was, nevertheless, necessary for Gladstone to appease in some way the Radical wing of his party, in order to retain its continued support. Radicals did not approve coercion, and their sympathies were all with the oppressed of Ireland (as were Gladstone's own in many ways). During his second tenure of power Gladstone was able to meet some of their wishes, along lines that had been foreshadowed in his reform measure just after Palmerston's death.

Chapter Eleven

Reform and Egypt
(1883–5)

THE subject of democracy and its justifications
must have been impressed on Gladstone's mind
by his Government's unhappy experiences over the
Transvaal question during its first winter in power.
In his Midlothian speeches Gladstone had coupled
the Transvaal, annexed in 1877, with Cyprus, and
said that he regarded both acquisitions to the empire
as valueless. The Boers, the Dutch inhabitants of the
Transvaal, therefore expected that they would regain
their independence as soon as he resumed office; an
independence that they were the more free to enjoy
since the Zulu War had disposed of their greatest
local enemy and the Zulu king had been deported.
Gladstone, however, preferred first to investigate a
plan for a South African federation of some kind,
and the summer and autumn of 1880 were consumed
in disputes, in South Africa and between Cape Town
and London, about the form that such a federation
should take. The Boers lost patience, and in December
took up arms to assert their right to govern themselves. General Colley, who was sent against them
with a small force, lost a number of minor actions,
ending with that of Majuba (27 February 1881).

That Majuba was certainly a British defeat was

much clearer to the London public than was the insignificance of its scale—the British dead numbered only ninety-three, but Colley was among them, and the event was held to be disgraceful. Newspapers called for an expedition to wipe out the disgrace. Gladstone took the defeat in another mood : he accepted it as a reminder that the Boers wished earnestly to be independent, and he had the courage to oppose countermeasures that would necessarily cost lives. Bright and Chamberlain supported his view. He was magnanimous enough to agree at once to the main Boer demands, and to treat with the citizens of a distant province as if they were the inhabitants of a great and equal power. The convention of Pretoria (2 August 1881) gave back to the Transvaal entire independence except in the conduct of its relations with other states[1]; the Transvaal recognised British 'suzerainty' in return. Three years later a new convention which modified these arrangements slightly was made, omitting the word 'suzerainty' : an omission that was later the cause of much misunderstanding and helped to bring about the Boer War of 1899–1902. What helped even more to make this war possible was the mistaken conclusion that the Boers drew from British readiness to sign the Pretoria convention of 1881. Like the Land Leaguers, the Boers misinterpreted Gladstone's magnanimity as weakness; they regarded the convention, as the Land Leaguers regarded the Land Act, as a concession extorted by force from a failing power, and though they did not take instant advantage of what they believed to be decadence, they treasured in their minds the picture of Great Britain as a feeble

[1] No supervision of Transvaal relations with the neighbouring independent Boer republic of the Orange Free State was demanded.

Goliath who could be overthrown whenever it suited the Boers to shake off a supervision they distrusted.

What connexion had these events with Gladstone's opinions on democracy?

The opinion in London that expressed itself vociferously in favour of attacking the Boers and taking revenge for Majuba was not, he was sure, the soundest opinion in the country. It is true that he always tended to mistrust the many opinions that did not agree with his own; but the longer his experience of politics extended, the more he felt that the opinion of 'Society' had little to recommend it by comparison with the opinion of ordinary men. He was so sure that he was right to stop the war in the Transvaal that the proper solution to the difficulty raised by strong feeling in some quarters at home seemed to him to be the widening of the electorate rather than the sending of an expeditionary force.

For the time being Ireland, and then Egypt (which will be discussed in a moment), kept him too busy to attend to the further reform of Parliament that he thought was called for. When at the turn of 1882–3 these turbulent countries seemed for a while not to demand the whole of his attention, he could take up once more the question of reform. So far his government had done little that its Radical supporters wanted, except for abolishing flogging in the armed services, and allowing Dissenters to hold their own burial services in Church of England graveyards, and tenants of land to shoot rabbits. In 1883 Gladstone sanctioned and encouraged the passing of an effective Corrupt Practices Act, a measure that finally put an end to the indignities of Eatanswill electioneering, and may be compared with the Ballot Act of 1872 as one of the laws that have done most to make Great Britain an efficient democracy. For the first time while Prime Minister he took no hand himself in the drafting of the major bill of a session, though he was none the less strongly in favour of the bill.

1883 marked another Radical triumph, on an important but peculiarly distasteful subject. In 1864 an Act was passed which, with some extensions in the next few years, set up in eighteen ports and garrison towns what amounted to a system of licensed and regulated prostitution, supervised by a special branch of Scotland Yard. Feeling against the system, as degrading to the women concerned and an excessive and illiberal extension of police power, was gradually worked up during the seventies.

On the political side this agitation secured as its leader James Stansfeld, an able Radical Nonconformist and a friend of Mazzini's, who had been a junior Cabinet Minister in Gladstone's first government. This government often considered the subject, and even introduced a bill, without securing any action. Stansfeld had the parliamentary skill needed to forward the fortunes of the movement in the House of Commons. There was no room for him in the Cabinet of 1880—the growing brilliance of Chamberlain outshone all other Radicals—and, so that he might devote himself to the cause he had made his own, he refused a kindly worded offer from Gladstone that he should be proposed as Deputy Speaker. He knew that Gladstone sympathised with him, but the Prime Minister's attention was not concentrated on the same aspect of the problem. Ever since his twenties Gladstone had devoted himself, under an arrangement made with one or two friends that each should devote part of his time and income to bettering the lot of some class of unfortunates, to strenuous efforts for reclaiming prostitutes from the streets and persuading them to some other way of life. These efforts he pursued with an ingenuous disregard for what London would think of the sight of his well-known figure talking to one of them at a corner of Coventry Street. (On one occasion, while he was Chancellor of the Exchequer, a man who saw him thus in conversation came up and tried to blackmail him; Gladstone gave him in charge at once, and the man was duly sentenced. Some months later Gladstone intervened with the Home Secretary to secure his early release from prison before he had served a quarter of his term.) Perfectly confident in his own integrity, perfectly convinced as a matter of faith that prostitution was wrong, Gladstone with his wife's help continued this work to the end of his life. To some people it seemed an eccentricity, and it probably helped to earn him the distrust of the Queen.

However, these efforts were personal only. Stansfeld hoped to make his attack on institutional rather than personal grounds; and by choosing his moment well, managed in April 1883 to persuade the Commons to pass a resolution condemning the relevant Acts. It was not until three years later, in another Parliament and under a Cabinet in which Hartington (his main Liberal opponent) had no voice, that he was able to secure the passage of an Act of repeal, which just managed to find its way (undebated) through both Houses before the long debate on Irish Home Rule got under way in 1886. Thus England was released from a harmful system; and in the light of English experience many similar systems abroad have also been abandoned.

The 1883 resolution on this subject and the Corrupt Practices Act were Radical gains of a kind. Next year, under pressure from Chamberlain at the top of his Radical form, Gladstone embarked on a more elaborate reform, of such importance as to demand his personal intervention at every stage. Radical feeling, in the Commons and the country alike, had pressed for some years for the extension to householders in the countryside of the vote which the Act of 1867 had provided for householders in the towns. The bill to secure this widening of the electorate from some 3,000,000 to some 5,000,000, or nearly one in six of the whole population, passed the Commons fairly easily; but when it reached the Lords it was set on one side, by a motion that the necessary redistribution of seats should first be effected. Disraeli, not long before his death in April 1881, had recommended to the young Balfour that this tactic would best kill such a bill, since the problems of redistribution would raise so many local animosities within the Liberal party that, divided hopelessly against itself, the party would fall apart. The result was not as the old man's hopeful sagacity had foreseen.

Parliament was prorogued, and Chamberlain in a series of violent speeches in the country proclaimed that the Lords must 'bend or break'. Gladstone foresaw another crisis which might equal in gravity that of 1832, unless some accommodation could be reached between the two houses and the two parties, and appealed at the end of August to the one quarter whence he knew that the Conservative party would listen to advice: the Crown. We have seen already that the Queen's attitude to him by this time was reserved at the warmest, and their copious correspondence had abounded since 1880 in warnings and expostulations on her side, met on his with courteous patience and with expositions that must have seemed tedious to her after Disraeli's brilliant political sketches. Once, in January 1883, Gladstone burst out to Rosebery, walking in the garden at Hawarden, that 'the Queen alone is enough to kill any man'. This was the only break in the iron reserve behind which he masked, outside his family circle, his harassing relationship with the Head of the State.

The Queen and Gladstone both saw that the difficulty in 1884 was too grave for personalities to stand in the way of settlement. He sent her a lengthy analysis of the problem; she mastered her resentment at the attacks on the Lords, and reported herself 'much struck by the fairness and impartiality' of her Prime Minister's paper. She caused Gladstone's reasonable arguments to be circulated among leading figures of the Opposition, and appealed to Salisbury and Gladstone to meet and talk the trouble over. Party passion was inflamed to an unusual degree. The subject of redistributing seats in the Commons inevitably makes the great English parties suspect each other; for neither side wants to believe that the other will handle the question with honesty, and each dislikes proposals made from across the House because it fears them to be biased, even if unconsciously, in its opponents' favour. 'The whole operation' of private talks, as Gladstone wrote to Bright, 'is essentially delicate and slippery', but it was carried through. Over tea in Downing Street, Salisbury and Northcote were told by Gladstone of the Government's proposals for altering constituencies, before they were made public. The leaders of the two parties each recognised in the other his intellectual equal, and they speedily reached agreement. The franchise bill was passed at the end of 1884, and the redistribution bill next year.

Three points in this settlement were of political significance, besides the statesmanlike moderation on both sides that had brought it about. It trebled the Irish electorate. Parnell observed in sardonic silence the quarrel of the two great parties he hated, knowing that if it could be resolved he would be master of Ireland. Secondly, it abolished all the remaining small boroughs with less than 15,000 voters; and third, it divided up most of the old two-member constituencies in town and country alike. This last proposal was made not by Radicals but by Conservatives, on grounds of electoral convenience rather than abstract principle. Salisbury assented to it, for he felt that in the long run his party would gain from the conservatism of the English countryside. In the short run, it was the Radicals who gained, for the abolition of most two-member seats ended the practice of running a Whig and a Radical in double harness against a pair of Conservatives, and the Whigs soon ceased to be a branch of the Liberal Party.

The franchise crisis in 1884 was complicated by a crisis in foreign affairs at the same time, over a question than which only the Slesvig-Holstein difficulty presented a more intricate series of problems to the diplomats of the century, the question of Egypt. To understand it we must again look back for a moment. The Suez Canal, built by French engineers with

French capital, and opened in 1869, had much increased the ease and volume of European trade with India. It had also much increased the political importance of Egypt, still a province of the vast Turkish empire, governed by a Khedive subordinate to the Sultan at Constantinople.

The Egyptian Government had trouble in administering the affairs of the canal. By a daring coup, Disraeli secured in 1875 the purchase for the British Government of the Khedive's shares, 44 per cent. of the total capital of the canal company. Gladstone thought the coup too daring, and did not approve its financing through private channels, without parliamentary sanction, but the country gladly accepted the increase in British power. In 1876 Disraeli had to agree to joint Anglo-French intervention in Egypt's confused finances, and three years later a formal 'Dual Control' over the Egyptian treasury was set up.

The Egyptians gradually developed anew a conception of their own nationality, which late in 1881 took precise political form as a revolt headed by Arabi Pasha, an army officer, against the authority of the Khedive. The many foreigners attracted to Egypt by the canal were unpopular there, and in June 1882 some of Arabi's followers, rioting in Alexandria, caused considerable loss of life in the European colony. Some fifty foreigners of various nationalities were killed, and the powers of the Dual Control had to send their fleets to stand by and protect the survivors. Gladstone did everything that he could to get other help as well, so that any intervention would be made by the Concert of Europe and not by England and France alone, but no other power would stir, and in the end even the French withdrew. The British fleet was left facing the Alexandrian rioters, who were constructing batteries to fire upon it, and who believed in nothing but force and could only be compelled by force to desist. Therefore on 11 July 1882, Alexandria was bombarded by the British and the batteries were silenced. This drove John Bright from Gladstone's Cabinet. He had always found it difficult to justify the use of force, even for ends that he thought worthy, and in this case he found it impossible, for he mistrusted the purposes of our intervention in Egypt. (He never held office again.)

His resignation raised no serious difficulty, unlike an external problem which came up at the same time. The French were angry at having failed to take part in our success at Alexandria, and still more angry when a small British expeditionary force under Wolseley landed in Egypt, annihilated Arabi's army, and captured its leader at the battle of Tel-el-Kebir (13 September). The French saw Egypt, which they had regarded for nearly a century as a zone of influence of their own, and which contained in the canal one of the marvels of modern French engineering, pass under the control of their neighbour and hereditary enemy. That it was their own fault that action had been taken by Great Britain alone and not in amicable concord with themselves made their sense of grievance no less acute.

The measures into which Gladstone's Government was inevitably drawn after the military occupation of Egypt were much affected by this French hostility. Gladstone could never look at foreign problems with the single eye of a British patriot : he saw them always in their European context, and tried to solve them in the way that would be best not only for his own country but for Europe as a whole. Pursuing these ideas, with the assistance of the failing Granville, he secured in 1885, after three years' negotiation, a settlement of the Egyptian debt. This placed the finances of the country, and hence control of its administration, under a board composed of the six European great powers. Thus Gladstone satisfied at once his humanitarian feelings, disliking riots, and his treasury principles, disliking waste. Two of the six powers, however, France and Russia, could be relied on to oppose any British proposal. They could only be out-voted if Germany and Austria-Hungary took the British side. The necessity to secure German help (Austria-Hungary normally voted as Germany suggested) as a condition of the good government of Egypt placed unforeseen traps in the way of British diplomacy for a generation to come. It was ingenuous of Gladstone to suppose that Bismarck would not take the advantage thus held out to him. As it was, Bismarck made many difficulties while the settlement was under negotiation; for European, not imperialist, purposes he wanted to tease the British into giving him an African colony. Modern German statesmen have never been averse to grasping levers that enable them to exert a control over the actions of other countries, and the greatest of them was hardly more immune from the temptation to seize such a lever than the least. For the next nineteen years Gladstone's Egyptian settlement served to keep England and France apart. But the settlement had been composed in all innocence by a man who sought the unity and not the division of Europe, and who never regarded the British occupation of Egypt as likely to last long.

Other powers expected that England, once in Egypt, would declare herself formally the protecting power and establish a permanent garrison. No policy could be farther from the intention of the man who had denounced Disraeli for making England the protecting power in Cyprus. Gladstone saw the occupation of Egypt as a temporary necessity, to secure the population from military excess and to safeguard the rights of the shareholders in the canal. He regretted it, and had no desire to retain a military footing there. But developments in the Nile valley forced him, step by step, down a path of tragedy.

As soon as British administrators, few in number but strong in ability, with Sir Evelyn Baring (later Lord Cromer) as their chief, arrived in Egypt, they began the cleansing of an Augean Stable of dirt, disease, and crime. Serious efforts were made to stamp out the trade in slaves, which was still being conducted, across the Red Sea, with the interior of an African continent much of which remained to be explored. But already before Tel-el-Kebir a new movement far up the Nile had begun to show signs of its existence, and by the autumn of 1883 it began to threaten the security of Egypt itself. This movement was at bottom religious, and its fanatical head took the title of Mahdi ('he who is guided aright'), the expected Messiah of the Moslem world.

Unfortunately information about the Mahdi and his followers was hard to come by in London or even in Cairo. In November 1883 an Egyptian army 10,000 strong under an English colonel, Hicks, marched out into the desert to deal with him, and vanished; for some time the exact date and place of its destruction were uncertain. There were various

161

Egyptian garrisons scattered round the Sudan, and the British Government decided that they ought, if possible, to be withdrawn. The local authorities were not to be trusted; someone had to go out and report on the chances of getting them away. Hurriedly, in January 1884, someone also in his own way a fanatic was chosen to go and reconnoitre the Mahdi: Charles Gordon, an eccentric General of Engineers, who knew the Sudan—of which he had been Governor-General in 1877-9—and had acquired a popular reputation as a fearless Christian soldier from his exploits in China in the sixties.

Gladstone never himself met Gordon, for he was ill in the country at the moment when a Cabinet committee under Hartington interviewed the general and commissioned him to go out to Khartoum and report on the evacuation of the 32,000 Egyptian troops in the area. But as Prime Minister, Gladstone was ultimately responsible for the decision to send him, for all the decisions that had thereafter to be taken, and for the delays that occurred before they were arrived at. No action in his life, not even his declaration in favour of Irish Home Rule, was as unpopular as his apparent failure to support a national hero at a post of danger. It earned him a stinging rebuke from the Queen (sent by telegram in clear instead of the customary cipher), it cost his party office, and it helped to weaken them severely at the next election. Yet his action was less inexcusable than it seemed to his contemporaries, who did not know how badly he and Gordon were informed, through no faults of their own, of each other's intentions.

A few weeks after Gordon reached Khartoum in February 1884, the telegraph that connected Khartoum and Cairo was cut by the Mahdi's forces, and thereafter the General could communicate with his superiors only intermittently and by messenger. Neither he nor the Prime Minister ever seem to have understood quite how thoroughly cut off from each other they were, and neither altogether trusted the judgement of a man he had never met. Some of Gordon's messages, when they became known in London, alarmed Liberals by their bellicose tone, and some of Gladstone's fine-spun instructions when they reached Khartoum seemed to Gordon, who did not get them either complete or in correct order, to be mere prevarications. Moreover, neither of them appreciated properly the nature or significance of the Mahdist movement, and they misunderstood it in different ways. Gordon thought that it was merely a gang seeking after power, like the gangs of slavers with whom he had dealt on the upper Nile a few years before.[1] Gladstone thought that the movement was political in a better sense, and spoke of the Sudanese as 'people . . . struggling rightly to be free'. The result of what had been intended as a reconnaissance by a single officer was a powerful expedition up the 1,600 miles of river that separate Cairo from Khartoum, to try to bring that officer away. The decision to send Wolseley's force up the Nile was finally taken in August 1884. Wolseley took too much trouble to ensure its safe transit, when rapid transit was what mattered most. On 28 January

[1] He asked to have one of his former enemies, an able Arab slave dealer called Zebehr, sent down to help him after he reached Khartoum. This proposal was abhorrent to Liberals of all shades, and was refused, though Gladstone said characteristically that he thought (had he not again been ill) he could have persuaded the Commons to agree to it.

1885, an advance party in one of Gordon's own steamers, delayed for two days by a general's indecision, reached Khartoum, to find it was two days too late. The Redcoats were fired on from Gordon's palace : Gordon was dead.

Bitter recriminations broke out in London, Conservatives attacking Gladstone for not sending help sooner and Radicals attacking him for sending it at all. Someone reversed the initials by which the Grand Old Man of the Liberal party was already known, and said that they meant Murderer of Gordon. The last word may be left with Gladstone, who said in debate :

> 'We had no alternative in this Egyptian policy. Each step was inevitable; our decisions, sad and deplorable as they may have been in themselves, were yet inevitable in the circumstances, and at the moment when we were called upon to undertake them.'

He told Bright afterwards that he had been 'tortured' by the whole affair.

Chapter Twelve

Home Rule
(1885–6)

THE failure of the attempt to relieve Gordon doomed the Government. Yet before it fell it had a last chance to apply the doctrines which it had been elected five years earlier to put into practice. The Russian authorities, observing that British attention was concentrated wholly on the valley of the Nile, thought the moment auspicious for a move in the valley of the Oxus. All through the second half of the century, while British dominion was spreading over Africa, Russian power was being extended into central Asia; and Russian penetration had now begun to approach the frontiers of Afghanistan. The Government of India was alarmed; in response to protests from it, Granville engaged in discussions with the Russian Government about the northern frontier of Afghanistan, discussions that were long protracted while Russian officers were busy occupying the areas in dispute. At the end of March 1885, Russian and Afghan troops clashed at the remote border village of Penjdeh, and though the Amir of Afghanistan, who was visiting India at the time, did not take this 'frontier scuffle' seriously, the anti-Russian chorus in England clamoured for war on Afghanistan's behalf.

On 27 April Gladstone asked the Commons, in an

ingenious and effective speech, for a vote of credit of £11,000,000 to meet Russian aggression if need arose, and secured unanimous approval. Simultaneously he and Granville proposed to Russia, not war but arbitration; the proposal was accepted and the danger passed away. The incident showed how correct had been Gladstone's Afghan policy in the Midlothian campaign: had the British continued a 'forward' policy many Afghans would have welcomed the Russian advance, and war with Russia would have been much more probable. It also showed the value of arbitration in quarrels between states, a value that Gladstone had learned from Aberdeen in the forties and stressed to his own cost in the *Alabama* settlement. Though the Commons only supported his Afghan policy by 290 against 260 in a debate in May 1885, that policy was thankfully executed by his successors in office.

In a letter to his wife on 1 May, Gladstone described the recent history of his Cabinet as 'a wild romance of politics, with a continual succession of hairbreath escapes and strange accidents pressing upon one another'; there were more and more threats of resignation as spring turned to summer and as it became clear that continued disorder in Ireland required a policy on coercion. In this most restive and effervescent parliamentary decade of the century, the situation in the Commons was no easier than in the Cabinet. Churchill, who had become one of the dominating figures in his party, extended to the Irish the hope that a Conservative Government would rule Ireland without any Coercion Act at all. In the May debate on Afghanistan it was noticed that some forty Irish members voted against Gladstone, and on 8 June the combination of Irish with Conservative votes against a Budget which did not attract much Radical support put the Government into a minority of twelve. Shaftesbury (who died that autumn) called this 'an act of folly amounting to wickedness. God is not in all their thoughts, nor the country either. All seek their own, and their own is party-spirit, momentary triumph, political hatred, and the indulgence of low, personal, and unpatriotic passion'. Gladstone may privately have felt the same, but he remembered his own part in defeating Disraeli's Budget in 1852, and was sure that he ought to resign. There could be no election until the winter, owing to the revision of the register which had to follow the redistribution of seats. Salisbury agreed, after hesitation, to hold office for the time being with a 'caretaker' Conservative Government in which Churchill's personality secured for himself the Secretaryship of State for India. Salisbury took over the Foreign Office as well as the duties of Prime Minister.

Gladstone was by now wholly preoccupied with the Irish question, so far as a man of such multifarious interests could ever be preoccupied with one single subject. Long meditation had brought him to conclude that an answer to it could only be found by the grant to the Irish of extensive powers of self-government, with some kind of Irish authority in Dublin that was responsible to the Irish electors in place of the English authority that answered only to the Crown and the Cabinet at Westminster. As long ago as 1871 he had guarded himself in private against a suggestion that his views did not embrace such a programme of 'Home Rule'; later experience of

Ireland, especially in the difficult three years since his nephew Cavendish's murder, had convinced him that the only way out of the Irish labyrinth, which had the fact of conquest at its foundation, was to break that foundation up and admit that the Irish had the right to govern themselves.

Before he left office, he had begun to hint pretty strongly to this effect to some of his colleagues. But when a combination between Irish and Conservative M.P.s brought his Government down, he naturally paused to see what would come of it. He knew there was only one thing that the Irish wanted, Home Rule; he could not conceive that their representatives would act with the Conservative party unless they felt that Home Rule might result from the co-operation. He knew that the citadel of the Conservative political fortress was the overwhelming Conservative majority in the House of Lords. That majority would not bow to the wishes of any party but its own unless it was faced with revolution as the alternative; but it would listen to its own leaders. Over half a century before, he remembered, it had listened to the Duke of Wellington and agreed to give Irish Roman Catholics full political rights. Over half a century before, again, the Lords had agreed—by a slender majority—to pass the great Reform Bill, when refusal would certainly have meant the creation of some sixty Whig peers and might have meant revolution as well. In 1846, still under Wellington's personal influence, they had agreed to the repeal of the Corn Laws, and in 1867 Disraeli had persuaded them to consent to a further measure of parliamentary reform.

Gladstone had often come into conflict with the

Lords himself; the latest difficulty, over redistributing seats, had still not been quite settled in June 1885 when he left office (the measure passed a few days later). He knew that since his attacks on Disraeli's Eastern policy in the seventies Court opinion had set firmly against him, and that Court opinion counted for much among the peers; he knew that party opinion counted for more, and that Conservatives had never forgiven him for organizing the downfall of 'Beaconsfieldism' in the Midlothian campaign. He concluded therefore that the best hope for an Irish settlement was that it should be worked out between the Irish and the Conservative leaders, preferably in private; the last thing he wanted was for it to become a matter of day-to-day political strife between parties. As he said to Rosebery at Easter : 'I am sick of contention : I cannot at my age spend the rest of my life in contention.' He has often been criticised for saying so little at this time about the completion of his own conversion to Home Rule, and for doing so little to carry colleagues with him, on the grounds that it did harm to the Liberal party when the project for Home Rule was thrust before it suddenly in December. This criticism overlooks Gladstone's attempt at the time to keep this most delicate and awkward problem out of party politics altogether, which made secrecy about his own views essential and consultation with colleagues unnecessary.

The need for silence he interpreted strictly : he would not enter into any communication with the Irish, for he felt that it was improper for the two great English parties to embark on any kind of competition for Irish votes, either at the coming election or in the new Parliament. Parnell remained in the dark about Gladstone's intentions, in spite of private inquiries through Mrs. O'Shea, and was deliberately misled by O'Shea about Chamberlain's; so in the end, just before the elections began in November, he told the Irish in England to vote Conservative. This action is thought to have raised the Conservative strength in the new House of Commons by some twenty or twenty-five at least—a difference of forty or fifty votes in a division. Parnell, though he knew nothing of Liberal intentions, had firm reasons for believing in Conservative support. At a secret meeting in August 1885 Carnarvon, Salisbury's Viceroy of Ireland, had given him reason to believe that the Conservative party would not look unkindly on a project of Home Rule, and though Salisbury later repudiated Carnarvon, he knew of the conversation at the time and must have been aware of the Viceroy's attitude.

Salisbury's position this autumn was awkward in several ways. He headed a Government with no majority in the Commons and with the certainty of elections in a few months' time. Though he was Prime Minister, Churchill's extremely rapid rise to eminence must have warned him that a challenge to his own position might shortly be expected; was indeed delayed only by Churchill's preliminary struggle for the leadership in the Commons, already almost in his grasp. As Prime Minister, Salisbury believed in giving his colleagues free rein, to a much larger extent than Peel or Gladstone used to do : 'People make a distinction', he said once to his son, 'between principles and details, but the distinction is only valuable as an intellectual assistance. In practice, everything is done by the arrangement and execution of the details.' Therefore, he concluded, Ministers should look after the details in their own departments; therefore Carnarvon, once chosen, should have his head over Ireland. Carnarvon was as old a political friend of Salisbury's as Spencer was of Gladstone's, but their views on Irish policy were not closely enough in accord. Salisbury recalled how they had both resigned in 1867 rather than consent to the reform bill that Disraeli was ready, at a sacrifice of Conservative principle, to accept. What Gladstone remembered about 1867 was that the Lords had passed this bill; what Salisbury remembered was that he himself had moved its rejection. This precedent told in the new Prime Minister's mind against a change of front on Ireland towards which neither interest nor principle inclined him and against which the hearts of many of his staunchest supporters were set.

Salisbury once criticised Disraeli, severely but not altogether unjustly, as 'a statesman whose only final political principle was that the party must on no account be broken up'. Yet when Home Rule held out to Salisbury the temptation to behave as Peel had done in 1846, Carnarvon, recording several private talks with him about it, found that 'his main objection to any such proposals was his fear of repeating the conduct of Sir R. Peel at the time of the Corn Law Repeal. In addition to this, he was so engrossed with the management of the Foreign Office that it was with very great difficulty that any other subject could be brought before him'. Moreover, he could see at his elbow Churchill, obviously cast to play again forty years later the role of Disraeli (without Disraeli's handicap of being nobody's cousin) and lead a party revolt against an unreliable leader.

Among the most acute of the home problems that pressed for Salisbury's attention was the campaign which Chamberlain was conducting for what Goschen nicknamed the 'unauthorised programme' of the Liberal party, in a series of speeches even more vigorous than those of the previous year. What he was trying to do was to rouse in the countryside the same sort of radical feelings that Bright had stirred up in the towns with the reform agitation of the sixties, and to ensure that the country householders who had just been given a vote used it, not as Squire directed, but as their own common sense and their own interests urged them. Therefore he laid most stress on a proposal that local bodies should be set up (this was before the days of county councils) with powers to purchase and distribute land in allotments and smallholdings in such a way as to equip every farm labourer with 'three acres and a cow'. Free schools, and reform of the taxes so that their burden should lie more on the rich and less on the poor, were the other two points that he stressed, though he also touched—to Salisbury's horror—on Church disestablishment. He set out in September, on a tour of Scotland, to begin to put his views before the two million new voters, to most of whom 'three acres and a cow' were likely to appeal. In the next three months he made twenty great speeches, which gradually became milder in tone as the election approached (not an uncommon feature in English electoral campaigns, when each party hopes at the last moment to attract the votes of moderate men).

When the results began to be announced in November—the boroughs, as was then usual, *seriatim* and some days in advance of the counties—Birmingham and Glasgow alone of the large towns were solidly Liberal. Elsewhere there were numerous Conservative gains, and the Whigs were not slow to blame Chamberlain in private for having frightened good Churchmen away with his proposals for disestablishment. But Chamberlain, though he had spoken in towns, had not spoken for townsmen, and with the county results came his justification in the shape of a run of Liberal victories which gave the Liberals a majority of over three to two in the counties of Great Britain. In Ireland, on the other hand, not a single Liberal was returned, and Parnell's party won 85 of the 89 seats it contested, usually by large majorities. The figures would have been laughable in a less tragic context. The Liberals had in all 86 more seats than the Conservatives. The election of one Parnellite M.P. for Liverpool brought the total of Parnell's party up to exactly the same figure, 86.

Parliament was not to meet for some weeks, and Salisbury rightly determined to remain in office; there was no clear verdict of the electorate to justify any other course. Gladstone remained in the country, the silent object of the political curiosity of the nation. Quite late in the year his final withdrawal from politics had been regarded as possible; he was very old, and his voice had been giving him trouble. In the end he stood for Midlothian again, and was returned by a vote of more than two to one. His thoughts were concentrated on the Irish problem, in its European perspective; he was prepared to put personal convenience and personal glory aside, for the sake of a settlement that would give the Irish what they wanted without the sacrifice of any essential English interest. He was ready to return to office if that seemed necessary for Ireland, but meanwhile he wanted to lie low, in the hope that the Conservatives and the Irish would come to some public agreement that he could recommend his Liberal followers to support.

He always enjoyed his months at Hawarden, where he spent every moment that he could. It is always to be remembered, as the permanent background of his career from 1839 until his death, that he rejoiced in a perfectly happy marriage with a shrewd and humorous woman from whom he kept no secrets and who never passed on a secret that was confided to her. It is not impossible that the happiness of his home, combined with the great simplicity of his character, which was complex only on the surface, led him sometimes to be too ingenuous in his dealings in politics, where all men's motives could not be reckoned unselfish as he knew his own to be. He was wrong, for instance, to attribute to Salisbury in this autumn of 1885 a single-minded preoccupation with Ireland similar to his own; Salisbury had too many other things to think about, and knew that his associates included men anxious for power and consumed by ambition.

Ironically, it was from within Gladstone's family circle that the blow was struck which ruined his attempts to keep Home Rule out of politics. When he had originally stood for Midlothian, the Leeds seat, which he refused, had been accepted by his youngest son Herbert, who held it for thirty years. Herbert Gladstone knew exactly how his father's mind was moving on the Irish issue, and had built up over five years in Parliament extensive political friendships of his own on what might be called the left centre of the Liberal party. He was himself an ardent Home Ruler *de fide*. He knew that Chamberlain had visited Hawarden in October and had failed to reach a thorough understanding with his father. Herbert Gladstone believed, from what his friends told him and from what he could discern for himself, that some Radical leaders, of whom he thought Chamberlain and Dilke the chiefs, were contemplating breaking away from the Whigs and Gladstonian Liberals, to create a parliamentary faction with a Radical programme that would not include Home Rule. The Liberal newspapers, with several of which young Gladstone—unlike his father, who mistrusted the Press—was in touch, seemed to be veering towards such views and against friendly consideration for the Irish. Therefore he went up to London in December 1885, without saying anything of his intentions, to see some of his political and journalistic friends and warn them about the disaster which he saw impending over the Liberal party. Most unfortunately, he did not take enough care to ensure that what he said was, as he meant, regarded as entirely private. He spoke freely of Gladstone's and his own ideas on the necessity of Home Rule, and with some pungency of both Whig and Radical leaders. On 17 December most of what he had said appeared in print as his father's own view, and the secret of Gladstone's conversion was out. A denial issued at Hawarden was so obscurely worded as to confirm any doubts that remained.

Home Rule had now got into politics. It is true that Salisbury had already made up his mind to oppose it, so that it had no chance of passing the House of Lords. But Salisbury's hold on his own party was still uncertain, and what amounted to his opponent's declaration in favour of Home Rule confirmed against it those of Salisbury's followers who might have been tempted to toy with the project had any hand but Gladstone's been raised to bless it. While his son was in London, Gladstone told Salisbury's nephew Balfour that he still hoped for, and would support, a Conservative project of Home Rule. He need not have troubled to make an offer, which a Peel would have accepted, but which Salisbury had determined to refuse on grounds of principle and expediency alike.

The new House of Commons assembled in the middle of January 1886. Gladstone in his speech on the address advised his friends, 'as an old parliamentary hand' (a phrase that gave much unintended offence), to make no move for the time being, but a crisis was at once brought on by the Conservatives' decision, announced on the afternoon of the 26th, to apply coercion to Ireland again. Gladstone thought that coercion was bound to make the Irish problem worse; and advantage was taken of an amendment brought forward that night by a minion of Chamberlain's on another subject to put the Government into a minority of 79. Salisbury resigned, and on 1 February Gladstone kissed hands as his successor.

The task of Cabinet-making which he now undertook for the third time was almost intolerably complicated by the Irish issue. As Morley remarked, 'The giant mass of secular English prejudice against Ireland frowned like a mountain chain across the track' that Gladstone hoped would lead both countries to a better understanding of each other and a calmer way of life. The Irish members themselves

176

did not seek office in London, which Gladstone would not in any case have offered. Many English and Scottish Liberals now felt that they could not join a Prime Minister who seemed prepared to offer the Irish an autonomous executive in Dublin. This was the issue on which nearly all the Whig peers severed their connexion with the Liberal party; this was the issue on which Hartington, Gladstone's colleague in four Governments stretching over more than twenty years, felt he had to break away.

When Gladstone saw each of the men whom he hoped to persuade to join him, he read out the following statement of what he wanted to do :

'I propose to examine whether it is or is not practicable to comply with the desire widely prevalent in Ireland, and testified by the return of eighty-five out of one hundred and three representatives, for the establishment by statute of a legislative body to sit in Dublin, and to deal with Irish as distinguished from imperial affairs; in such a manner as would be just to each of the three kingdoms, equitable with reference to every class of the people of Ireland, conducive to the social order and harmony of that country, and calculated to support and consolidate the unity of the empire on the continued basis of imperial authority and mutual attachment.'

For half the previous Cabinet this was too much to ask. Granville, Spencer, Kimberley, Rosebery, Acton, Ripon were the only able peers who stood by Gladstone, and Granville's adherence posed a delicate problem. Though he had handled the Penjdeh affair adroitly, he was rightly thought to be past his best, and the Queen insisted that the control of foreign affairs be kept out of his hands. Rosebery had already been warned that he was her favourite for the Foreign Office. He had endeared himself to Gladstone politically by offering to join the Cabinet as soon as news came of Gordon's death, and he conducted foreign business for six months with little incident. But what was to be done for Granville? Gladstone thought him too old a friend to be cast out of office altogether, and needed, in any case, everyone of any abilities whom he could find. He offered Granville the Colonies, an imposing office (carrying a salary of which Granville happened to be in temporary need), and Granville accepted it.

This kindness to an old companion, apparently of slight significance, turned out one of the gravest errors that Gladstone ever made. It was not that Granville's administration of the colonies was in any way unsound, or that he failed to go on exerting his great powers of tactful conciliation on all sorts of people. But the post should have gone to Chamberlain, who asked for it. Had he secured it, he would have been distracted from a damaging preoccupation with Ireland by the business of an office that already seemed attractive to him, and the unity of the Liberal party might have been better preserved. If Gladstone had been able to enter into partnership with Chamberlain, they might between them have managed to carry much of the programme that was reserved for the Liberal Governments of 1905–15, and they would certainly have brought to a head earlier the clash between Lords and Commons that was resolved by the Parliament Act of 1911. But differences of outlook, temperament, training, religion, made the partnership impossible. There was never any sympathy between the two. Gladstone never appreciated either the abilities or the importance of a man nearly thirty years his junior, misread his efficient manner as an insolent one, and mistrusted the natural ambition of a self-made, self-confident man for a great career. Chamberlain in return mistrusted Gladstone's excessive subtlety, which he thought insincere, and too easily saw Gladstone as the man whose political longevity kept him from the leadership of a great party and the post of Prime Minister.

Chamberlain joined the Cabinet for a few weeks, in charge of local government, but got no co-operation from a Prime Minister busy drafting his Government of Ireland Bill, and was able to do nothing towards the execution of his 'unauthorised programme'. Circumstances gradually drove him to co-operate with his principal opponent within the Liberal party, Hartington; though he exaggerated in retrospect his readiness to move in this direction when he told Parnell's biographer twelve years later that his attitude to Home Rule could be summarised simply thus, 'I wanted to kill the bill'. Unfortunately the Radical leader who agreed most nearly with Gladstone on the Irish issue, Dilke, was not able to act as intermediary between the Prime Minister and Chamberlain, with whom he had much influence, for the divorce case which ruined Dilke's career as a statesman came on for trial just as the Government was being formed, and Gladstone later included in a list of his own supporters the terse note 'Dilke (unavailable)'. The most illustrious Radical, Bright, was disinclined to take part in the Irish venture, which he judged to be perilous. He strongly distrusted the Irish Nationalists, and moreover realised, as Gladstone never did, that Ulster already presented a problem of special complexity.

But the total number of Radical dissentients from Gladstone's policy was not large. The leader of disagreement on the other wing of the party was Hartington, a man far more self-confident than Chamberlain, with the assurance that came from his place in a great family of great possessions. Politics was one of the normal occupations of a Cavendish, but not the only one; Hartington's time was spent more happily in the hunting-field or with a gun than in the council chamber, and he brought to politics the downright freshness of a countryman and a countryman's eye for practical detail. Gladstone's proposal to examine a scheme for Irish self-government necessarily involved, as Hartington saw at once, the submission of a plan to Parliament; he could not consent to hand over Ireland to men such as the murderers of his brother, and when Gladstone pressed him to join the new Cabinet he refused. 'I never can get on with him in conversation', he had written to Granville a few months before; this particular interview was comparatively agreeable, and did not diminish the real respect with which each of the two men regarded the other's ability, but it did not shake Hartington's resolution to stay out.

The other troubles of Gladstone's Cabinet-making were comparatively slight, though the Queen, making little attempt to hide her hostility to her new Prime Minister, made difficulties over Court appointments. Harcourt, though a Whig by descent and a personal friend of Hartington, was a political friend of Chamberlain, and as much of a Radical by disposition as a man could be who had spent five years as Home Secretary in a time as violent as the eighties, when problems of public order had been exacerbated by Irish dynamite. Yet he could see no objections in principle to Gladstone's proposal, and went to the Exchequer. He succeeded in enforcing the biggest reduction in service estimates since Gladstone's efforts in that direction in the sixties, and established himself as the second figure on the Liberal benches in the Commons.

With the help of Morley, a Radical journalist now in office for the first time as Irish Secretary, and through him of Parnell, Gladstone devised a scheme of Irish government which he presented to the Commons as a bill on 8 April, 1886. It proposed the devolution to an Irish Parliament and executive of power over all Irish affairs except for a list of reserved subjects, of which foreign affairs, defence, and customs were the chief; these were to remain under the Westminster Parliament, from which Irish members were to be excluded. Its debate lasted for exactly two months, in scenes of excitement for which no parallel could be found since the days of the great Reform Bill,[1] and at an unusually distinguished level of oratory and argument. Hartington in particular displayed in these weeks higher qualities of parliamentary character than most men had suspected could lie behind his superb, aloof exterior and his languid manner, for the struggle against his old chief forced him for the first time to exert his powers to the full. They turned out to be considerable.

Up to the last Gladstone hoped that he might carry

[1] 'Members came down at break of day to secure their places', said Morley; 'before noon every seat was marked, and crowded benches were even arrayed on the floor of the House from the mace to the bar.'

his bill, and to this end he made many concessions in debate. He had already separated the economic aspect of the problem into a distinct measure, a land bill which was introduced and then dropped. He knew that Parnell was dissatisfied with the financial clauses of his bill, and held out hope of amendment in committee. He held out to Chamberlain hope of a similar amendment to try to resolve the irresolvable dilemma of the Irish members at Westminster : the bill proposed that they should in future be excluded, which meant for Ireland 'taxation without representation' by the imperial parliament; but to include them would mean that they would have a voice in British affairs, and might decide the fate of imperial governments, over matters which in Ireland would lie within the competence of the Dublin Parliament and outside imperial control. He even hinted (at a party meeting, withdrawing much of what he said there in the House itself) that the bill might be held up for some months, or withdrawn, redrafted, and resubmitted in the autumn, if only it could pass its second reading. At a similar meeting, Chamberlain read out with telling effect a weighty letter of Bright's, which made the old leader's hostility to Gladstone's scheme clear. Finally, in the small hours of 8 June, the vote on the second reading was taken. The bill was defeated by 343 to 313, 93 Liberals voting against it and only 14 M.P.s being absent from the division.[1]

Gladstone could have resigned, but preferred the bolder course of asking for a dissolution and fighting

[1] O'Shea was one of the absentees. If Parnell had cast the Irish vote in English seats on the other side in the previous November, the bill would presumably just have been carried in the Commons. However, the presumption that it would have been rejected in the Lords is even more strong.

the issue out in the country. The Queen granted the dissolution in accordance with precedent, though she took strong exception to the active and unprecedented part which her first minister played in the election campaign. The tone of this campaign may be given by two brief extracts from the address with which Churchill successfully appealed to the electors of South Paddington :

'Mr. Gladstone has reserved for his closing days a conspiracy against the honour of Britain and the welfare of Ireland more startlingly base and nefarious than any of those other numerous designs and plots which, during the last quarter of a century, have occupied his imagination. . . . all useful and desired reforms are to be indefinitely postponed, the British Constitution is to be torn up, the Liberal party shivered into fragments.

'And why? For this reason and no other : To gratify the ambition of an old man in a hurry.'

Voting took place in July, and is generally thought to have registered a decisive majority against Home Rule. It certainly returned a House of Commons in which 'Unionists'—Conservatives, that is, and rebel Liberals of various shades combined—had a majority of 110 over Home Rulers of all nationalities. One hundred and twenty of these Unionists stood for seats so certainly in their favour that their election was not opposed. Ensor thinks that 'it now appeared how much more anti-home rule the country was than the house'. Some Unionists argued that to propose devolution so near to the heart of a great empire was to propose that empire's dissolution, and certainly the opinion of most European governments of the day was on those lines. Bismarck never offered Poland or Alsace what Gladstone offered Ireland, and Francis Joseph offered Austria-Hungary a system of dyarchy which fastened on a dozen subject races the yoke of Germans and Hungarians. Endless possibilities of dispute were also raised, for the serious audiences of the time, by the details of Gladstone's proposal. But a simpler and a more popular cry was available to his opponents—the appeal to English national sentiment and national pride. The tale of misunderstandings between England and Ireland was still not complete, and from a thousand platforms Unionist orators proclaimed that the Irish had demonstrated by their outrages and crimes that they were barbarians unfit even to be trusted with the governance of their own nasty selves. Whoever proposed an Irish Parliament, so this argument ran, proposed to remove from Ireland the beneficent influences of British culture and British order, and to condemn her—surely against her own true interests—to the rule of her own murderers and thieves. Much that was good, as well as much that was evil, in English imperialism was to be found on the Unionist side in this campaign; the sober doctrine of responsibility for under-developed peoples beside what Hobbes called long ago the 'perpetual and restless desire of power after power, that ceaseth only in death'.

In Ireland 85 members were again returned in favour of Home Rule, 65 of them unopposed. In the rest of the kingdom the position of the previous year was, broadly speaking, reversed. Birmingham was solidly Unionist, though Gladstonian Liberals did well in most, and won at least one seat in all, other large towns (Gladstone himself being returned unopposed for Midlothian). The urban workers of England, Wales, and Scotland were prepared to take on trust from Gladstone a plan for Irish government which they had not had time to consider fully, because he convinced them that to vote for it was to vote for an act of justice and friendship towards a country that we had wrongly oppressed, and also because they trusted his judgement and his integrity. But the country workers for whom he had secured the vote were less enthusiastic. What had brought them to the poll in the previous autumn had been the hope of 'three acres and a cow'; nothing had been done by either side towards realising that hope, and in 1886 many thousands of them abstained—nearly a million and a half fewer votes were cast than in the year before, and by no means all this figure is accounted for by the large increase in unopposed returns. The Liberal vote in the counties fell by nearly 600,000, and a large majority of the county members in the new Parliament were Unionists.

In votes, the Unionist majority was less than 100,000, out of nearly three million cast; but the Constitution takes no account of calculations of votes cast in the country, by national sections or as a whole, and demands that the Prime Minister should have the support of a majority in the Lower House. No one knew this better than Gladstone, who resigned with his Cabinet at the end of July.

He was left to consider whether the part of Peel in the crisis of 1846 had not been played, forty years later, by himself rather than Lord Salisbury; and he had not Peel's consolation, the triumph of the cause for which he fought.

Chapter Thirteen

The Last Act
(1887–98)

THERE were two factors in the political situation that worked in Gladstone's favour. One was his own indomitable courage. He was fond of discussing the parliamentary courage of his contemporaries, among whom he singled out Russell, Peel, and Disraeli as the bravest (he paid a graceful tribute in the Commons to Disraeli's distinction in this field after the latter's death). He possessed this quality himself in an abundance equal at least to any of them. No position of inferiority in the division lists was likely to turn him aside from pursuing what he believed to be a just policy. Secondly, he had a powerful weapon outside the House. Schnadhorst, Chamberlain's assistant in creating the Liberal party 'caucus' machine, disagreed with his chief over Home Rule, and brought the most elaborately developed electioneering device in England on to Gladstone's side. For the first time since 1830, the strength of the most liberal party in the Commons had fallen below 200. But that the Liberal party of the eighties consisted of much more than an uneasy coalition of Whigs and Radicals is shown by the presence in the new Parliament of 1886 of a hard Gladstonian core 191 strong, backed as has been shown by proportionately more considerable feeling in the country.

Gladstone hoped that in the course of such years as might be left him he could sway English opinion decisively towards Home Rule. Parnell shared this hope, and thought that Gladstone's success would offer Ireland her best hope from English politics. Meanwhile he urged on Salisbury's Government a sensible plan of his own to meet the troubles of the Irish peasantry, whose sufferings were aggravated by falling corn prices. He proposed that for two years landlords should be forbidden to evict tenants who could pay up half their arrears of rent. In August 1887 economic necessity forced the Government to adopt this proposal, but in September 1886 it was rejected, because no Unionist wanted to appear to accept any suggestion from Parnell. Under pressure of growing distress, the Irish adopted a 'Plan of Campaign' which refused to landlords higher rents than local opinion, expressed through peasants' associations, thought reasonable. The landlords' answer to the Plan of Campaign was more evictions. The peasants' answer to evictions was, as always, crime : boycotting,[1] arson, intimidation, attacks on cattle, and in extreme cases murder.

The Government's answer to crime was, as always, coercion : coercion applied with ruthless vigour by a new star in the political sky, Arthur Balfour. Balfour was Salisbury's nephew, known when he went to the Irish Office early in 1887 as a youngish, foppish, elegant idler, and his appointment was thought to be

---

[1] Boycotting was not necessarily criminal. It was named after Captain Boycott, who in County Mayo in 1880 was cut off from all social intercourse and all economic help by his poor neighbours because he would not receive rents at rates fixed by the tenants. In the end Ulstermen harvested his crops for him, under the protection of 900 soldiers.

a job. His uncle knew better. When Balfour left that Office in 1891 it was to become the Conservative leader in the Commons, marked out as Salisbury's successor. He displayed grit, logic, and daring that showed the previous general view of him to have been altogether mistaken, and managed by apt severity to kill the Plan of Campaign.

Yet his tactics were not always correct. Of one particular blunder, his immediate declaration in favour of the police after a fatal riot at Mitchelstown on 9 September 1887, which seemed to call for long and impartial inquiry, Gladstone took advantage, and coined the slogan 'Remember Mitchelstown', which was heard for years from Liberal platforms all over the kingdom. Coercion applied by the Liberals against agrarian crime, as such, had attracted some sympathy from English workmen who did not love Irish methods. But coercion applied by Conservatives against peasant organizations, to enforce landlords' views of fair rents against tenants', presented another problem. The tenants were fighting the sort of battle that the English workman, with a history of successful struggle over two generations to establish trade unions behind him, could understand and approve. In the four years after the first defeat of Home Rule, Anglo-Irish sympathy developed, as Gladstone and Parnell hoped that it would, and Gladstone's education of the electorate progressed. One example of his work in this campaign may be quoted, from a contemporary note of Morley's on a meeting at Birmingham in November 1888 :

'The sight of the vast meeting was almost appalling, from fifteen to seventeen thousand people. He spoke with great vigour and freedom; the fine

passages probably heard all over; many other passages certainly not heard, but his gesture so strong
and varied as to be almost as interesting as the
words would have been. The speech lasted an hour
and fifty minutes; and he was not at all exhausted
when he sat down. The scene at the close was absolutely indescribable and incomparable, overwhelming like the sea.'

The Conservative counter to this campaign was
ingenious. In the spring of 1887, to assist Balfour in
the passing of his coercion bill, *The Times* published
a series of articles entitled 'Parnellism and Crime'.
Their object was to demonstrate that the Irish
Nationalist party in Parliament was intimately connected with much less reputable and more extremist
organizations in Ireland, and that its leaders privately
approved the crimes which they publicly condemned.
In particular, a letter was published in facsimile, on
the day of the division on the second reading of the
bill, from which it appeared that Parnell thought
Burke's murder in Phœnix Park justified. Parnell denied the charge that day (18 April) in the House, but
took no legal action, for he knew that an Irish jury's
verdict would carry no weight in England and that
no English jury would pronounce in his favour, certain though he was that the letter was a forgery. In
July of the following year, during a libel action
brought by a Parnellite against *The Times,* the
Attorney-General—it was then the custom for law
officers to continue in private practice while in office
—read a number of other damaging letters reflecting
on Parnell's conduct, and this did sting the latter into
demanding an inquiry.

A Special Commission of three Unionist judges was
accordingly set up, with the help of that particularly

abrupt form of parliamentary closure the 'guillotine' (devised in the previous year to help Balfour's coercion bill through the Commons), to inquire into 'the allegations and charges made against Members of Parliament and other persons in the recent action'. A grand inquisition, in fact, was to sit on the whole of the Irish land agitation for the previous decade; and the inquisitors did not allow it to be argued before them that the agitation had been provoked by landlords' injustice. For months the Commission heard evidence, at wearisome length and in repellent detail. At last, in February 1889, it approached the question of the letters. The manager of *The Times,* adroitly handled by Asquith (who was made famous by this case—he had only just entered Parliament), revealed that he had bought the letters because he thought that they were the sort of letters that Parnell would have written, and had not at the time of purchase any other evidence that they were genuine. He never had a chance to bring before the Commission a handwriting expert who was satisfied that they were; for a few days later Piggott, a disreputable Irish journalist, confessed that he had forged them all, then fled the country, and committed suicide.

A year later the Commission issued its final report, but public opinion had already made up its mind, and the many findings that were damaging to the Irish cause were overlooked in view of the grand fact that Parnell, who had been said by a powerful newspaper, and believed by a powerful party, to be the friend and associate of murderers, had been the victim of a petty criminal and a great intrigue.

At the end of the year 1890, in which Gladstone's hopes for Home Rule seemed so bright now that the character of its chief Irish supporter had been cleared, that character received a new and far more serious blow. Parnell, having emerged with credit from the great intrigue, fell victim to a small one, and was ruined by his private life. His fall ruined also Gladstone's attempt to see immediate justice done to Ireland.

Ten years before, Parnell had met an English-woman, the deserted wife of an Irish colleague, O'Shea. They fell in love at once, and lived together thereafter, at her house at Eltham and in various watering-places, with the knowledge and connivance of O'Shea, who came down to Eltham occasionally in Parnell's absence to keep up appearances for the sake of Mrs. O'Shea's aunt, an old lady whose large fortune the niece expected to inherit. During this time she bore Parnell three children (one of them while he was in prison). They were entirely devoted to each other; but O'Shea would not divorce her, since he wanted a share of the aunt's money, and he used the position to extort a kind of blackmail from Parnell. He enjoyed politics, liked to be used as an inter-mediary—his friendship with Chamberlain had its effects on the Irish question, as has been seen—and forced Parnell to secure for him minor parliamentary advantages. When the aunt died, her will was con-tested by the rest of the family; and O'Shea, unable to lay his hands on a capital sum or to go on drawing the allowance that the aunt used to pay him, lost patience and brought an action for divorce, citing Parnell as co-respondent.

The hearing, long delayed, finally came on in November 1890. Parnell did not put in an appear-ance. Mrs. O'Shea very foolishly contested the suit, with denials and counter-accusations which she made no serious attempt to substantiate. The action thus gave her husband an opportunity to present the world with a picture of himself as a trusting and injured man, which, although it has since been proved by Captain Henry Harrison a gross distortion of the facts and untrue in almost every particular, served at the time to damage and discredit Parnell to such an extent that not only did the Roman Catholic and Nonconformist clergy alike demand his withdrawal from public life, but hundreds of thousands of English voters, irrespective of their opinions on the sanctity of marriage, felt that they had to reconsider their views on Home Rule; for Parnell seemed, through O'Shea's false witness, to have behaved so long with such duplicity in his private life that it would be madness to trust him to govern the affairs of his country.

Parnell should have retired for a while to let the sensation pass away. By the time that the Liberal party had again achieved power, he could have returned to the Irish leadership. But he was too proud to admit that he had antagonized for a time many powerful influences, in England and Ireland alike; he had long hated the secrecy in which he had had to shroud his relations with the woman he loved; and he thought that, since force of character had made him leader of the Irish party, force of character could keep him there. Therefore when Parliament met, a week after the divorce decree, he evaded messengers from Gladstone who sought to warn him of the need for withdrawal, and tricked his party into re-electing him its chairman.

This was foolish. It was equally foolish of Gladstone to sanction at once the publication of the letter of warning (nominally addressed to Morley) in which he described Parnell's continuance in leadership as probably 'productive of consequences disastrous in the highest degree to the cause of Ireland'. When what had been written as a private and friendly warning became at once a public document, it looked like a threat. Parnell now lost his head. Abandoned by the majority of his colleagues in Parliament, he published a savage attack on Gladstone for having, a year previously, suggested to him in private severe limitations on Home Rule which would have made it almost worthless. The charge was quite untrue, but served its turn; Parnell was now appealing to the wild and extreme elements in Irish nationalism which he had hitherto kept in check, in a hopeless attempt to foist the blame for the public effects of private disgrace on to the only English party which could offer support to his country's cause.

Gladstone could easily have retaliated on Parnell to rebut the personal attack on himself. But it came when he was, after a few days' reflection, more immune from the excited atmosphere of the House of Commons in which he had been impelled to publish his letter to Morley. Gladstone hated gossip, and had refused to believe the occasional rumours current in Society about the affair; and though he had no sympathy with what Parnell had done, he did not want to interfere unnecessarily in what he thought a purely Irish quarrel, and did not think it worth while to defend his own good name against Parnell's irresponsible charges that he had secretly been an enemy of Home Rule.[1] He did want, though, to pursue the

[1] Unfortunately for Gladstone's reputation in Ireland, Parnell's attack on him succeeded in lodging there for many years the impression that his support for the Irish cause had been at best half-hearted.

struggle for the better government of Ireland. 'I have not the slightest desire', Salisbury wrote in this year to Carnarvon, 'to satisfy the national aspirations of Ireland.' Gladstone by now desired little else. He desired it because he thought that it was best for distinct nationalities to live under the rule of their own nationals and not of foreigners; and also because he thought it was a debt of honour which England owed to Ireland after seven centuries of oppression, in atonement for Pitt's trickery which had secured the Act of Union in 1800. His enemies have often said that he desired only power, that he was insatiable of office, and craved to return to Downing Street. This is a ludicrous account of the motives of a man who, already within a few weeks of the age at which Palmerston succumbed to the cares of his relatively quiescent office, was prepared to engage in political battle with the Queen, with London Society, and with a powerful party of which he had himself once been a promising member. He was acting simply in pursuit of what he believed to be right; and the numerous comparisons which he made at this time between himself and Sisyphus, when the stone had rolled to the bottom of the hill, show that he had only the faintest hopes of success.

It was not, perhaps, altogether a disaster for Ireland that in October 1891 Parnell died suddenly; but his party remained split for many years after his death, until John Redmond knit it together again.

In order to make Home Rule palatable to a British electorate, it was judged necessary to offer the voters other inducements than the appeal to justice alone. Accordingly in the autumn of 1891 Gladstone was persuaded to agree to an extensive programme of reform, as much Radical as Liberal, which the Liberal party adopted officially in conference at Newcastle. Besides Home Rule, the list included land reforms, power for local bodies to forbid the sale of drink, triennial parliaments, 'one man one vote', elected parish councils (elected county councils had been set up by the Conservatives in 1888), and Church disestablishment in Wales and Scotland. (This last point Gladstone was most reluctant to accept, and he never himself urged it with any vehemence.)

In July 1892 this programme secured the Liberal party a small majority at a general election. Gladstone, who was returned by a few hundred votes for Midlothian, had hoped to do much better : as it was, there were only four more Liberal than Conservative M.P.s, and the rest of his majority came from the superiority of 81 Irish members (and one Labour) over the 46 Liberal Unionists, headed in the Commons by Chamberlain. In Great Britain a very slight, and in Ireland a large, majority of votes were cast in favour of Home Rule. Salisbury waited to meet Parliament, and was at once defeated there. In August Gladstone became Prime Minister for the fourth time.

Granville had died the year before. The Cabinet was an improvement on the one of 1886 in that it contained new men of promise, Asquith, Fowler, and Bryce, as well as the successful younger men of the previous Liberal Ministry, Rosebery, Morley, and Campbell-Bannerman. Most of its members were ambitious, and only loyalty to their chief kept their ambitions from disrupting the Government through their quarrels with each other. Harcourt's strong temper made him prominent in these dissensions.

Rosebery, back at the Foreign Office, displayed a prickly independence from his Prime Minister which pained the latter, but Rosebery's spirit was serviceable to England in the only foreign crisis of importance, a dispute with France in 1893 about the frontiers of Siam, in which France's more extreme claims on that country were defeated.

Gladstone pressed on with what he regarded as his Government's principal task, and in February 1893 introduced his second Home Rule Bill. Its provisions followed in general those of the 1886 bill, except that eighty Irish members were to remain at Westminster. After 82 days of debate, in which this 'old, wild, and incomprehensible man' (as the Queen described him when he took office) frequently took part although he could count even more years of age than the bill had days of debate, it passed its third reading in the Commons by 34 votes on 1 September. A week later the Lords, after four days' discussion, voted it down by 419 to 41, on the motion of Hartington (who had lately succeeded his father as Duke of Devonshire). The defeat was a heavy one, but the Home Rule cause gained greatly in the long run from the exhaustive study which was lavished on the bill during the committee stage in the Commons. All the many difficulties were thrashed out in public, and ways for their eventual solution were made clear.

Gladstone pressed his colleagues to agree to a dissolution, at which the Liberals' cry would have been that of 1910—'The Peers against the People'—but none of them would agree. They were getting some parts of the Newcastle programme enacted into law —Fowler's measure to secure parish councils was only the most important of a number of useful if comparatively minor reforms which this Government achieved.[1] As his party would not support him in a struggle against the Lords, Gladstone was anxious to retire. Increasing deafness, and cataract in both eyes, provided excuses; the real cause of his final retirement was more substantial.

During the quarrel with France over Siam, there was a naval scare in England, not unlike the 'Three Panics' of the fifties and sixties which Cobden had denounced in a once famous pamphlet of that title. It appeared that France and Russia combined might have in a few years' time more battleships than this country; the first diplomatic result of Bismarck's dismissal in 1890 (after twenty-eight years' continuous power), an alliance between France which he had kept isolated and Russia, was by 1893 beginning to seem likely.[2] Such an alliance at that time would presumably be hostile to England. Salisbury had been inveigled in 1887 into aligning this country secretly with Bismarck's Triple Alliance (Germany, Austria-Hungary, Italy), and though Rosebery repudiated the

---

[1] Another feature of this Parliament deserves to be recorded as an instance of Gladstone's generosity in politics. Randolph Churchill, the bane of the 1880-5 Cabinet, the author of the violent Paddington address, had spoiled his own political career by an ill-considered resignation from the second post in Salisbury's Government at the end of 1886. By 1893 he was already suffering from the disease that killed him two years later, and had difficulty in making himself understood in a House that grew restive, and emptied, when he was addressing it. His son records that 'in these days it was observed that Mr. Gladstone would always be in his place to pay the greatest attention to [Churchill's] speeches and to reply elaborately to such arguments as he had advanced'.

[2] A military arrangement had, in fact, been signed secretly in 1892. The formal alliance was concluded in the winter of 1893-4 and published a year later.

actual document concerned, he continued the policy. In order to meet the Franco-Russian naval threat the Admiralty insisted on laying down seven British battleships in 1894, which involved an increase in the naval estimates of over £3,000,000—about the total of the payment on the *Alabama* claims.

Gladstone when he heard of this proposal described it as 'mad and drunk'. He opposed it vehemently, but could not get anyone to stand by him in doing so. Spencer, as First Lord of the Admiralty, agreed with his subordinates there; the Cabinet stood by Spencer; Harcourt, on Milner's advice, had a plan ready for providing the necessary money by death duties.[1] Gladstone could not see why in his old age he should abandon the cause of economy that he had championed thirty years before. He did not recognise the existence of any serious danger to Great Britain from overseas; he had always thought heavy spending on armaments a mistake. He still thought it a mistake, and nobody could convince him that if France, Russia, or any other powers made that mistake, this country ought to follow their example. Palmerston was dead, but Palmerston's policies survived, in the age of which Rhodes and Jameson were typical figures. Gladstone had a record of achievement behind him sound enough for him to be able to retire, sooner than tarnish it at its close by acquiescence in a policy he had contested all his life.

[1] This plan worked well, and through its later extensions the greatest inequalities of wealth in England have been much levelled out. This success makes an interesting contrast with Lloyd George's handling of the problem of financing the eight battleships laid down in 1908; his budget of 1909 brought on the decisive quarrel between Lords and Commons, but his proposed new land tax was, in the end, quietly dropped.

On 1 March 1894, sixty-one years after his maiden speech in the Commons, he made his last speech there—a warning that the Lords' opposition to Liberal bills had produced 'a state of things, of which we are compelled to say that in our judgment it cannot continue'. Two days later he resigned.

The Queen did not ask his advice about his successor. In spite of the naval controversy, he would have named Spencer. Instead she chose Rosebery, who was Prime Minister for an unhappy sixteen months that brought him no joy save what came from a non-political triumph—his horses won the Derby two years running. Their victories did not improve his standing in the eyes of Nonconformist Liberals who thought horse-racing immoral. On 22 June 1895, sick of his colleagues' dissensions, he took advantage of an unimportant defeat in the Commons to resign. The election next month returned a Conservative majority of 152,[1] and the Conservatives retained office for the next ten years.

Gladstone spent part of his retirement in editing the works of the eighteenth-century moralist Bishop Butler, whom he used to name with Homer, Aristotle, and Dante as his teachers. He emerged into public life only thrice: he grumbled against a Welsh Church Disestablishment Bill in 1895, and spoke on the Eastern Question at Chester that year and at Liverpool in the following autumn. The latter occasion, 24 September 1896, was his last great public speech. In it he urged action on the appalling massacres perpetrated in Turkey against Armenians,

---

[1] Spender points out that this large change was secured by a turnover of under 250,000 votes in an electorate of 6,333,000.

which he described as 'the most terrible and most monstrous series of proceedings that has ever been recorded in the dismal and the deplorable history of human crime'. 'The ground on which we stand [he said] is not British, nor European, but it is human.' 'Had I the years of 1876 upon me', the brave old man said to one of his sons, 'gladly would I start another campaign, even if as long as that.' But he knew that he was too old, and waited calmly for death, which was not long in coming. Late in 1897 he fell ill. After months of suffering, he died on 19 May 1898.

Chapter Fourteen

Successors

EXAMPLES and precedents drawn from Gladstone's life still influence the history of England. The greatest living English statesman is inspired to emulate his own father's antagonist: Gladstone was still the leader of a great party, and the mover as Prime Minister of the most important bill of the decade, in his eighty-fourth year. Every Minister, every aspirant to Cabinet rank, every serious writer on political affairs, cannot fail to be affected by a career in politics, of such length and such variety, which closed only fifty-four years ago. The financier needs to consider Gladstone's views on economy and tariffs, the democrat and the aristocrat alike must weigh his opinions on the franchise; and though the classical scholar may smile at his views on Homer, and the Churchman as well as the agnostic can leave unread his pages of theological controversy, the student of the world outside this country ignores at his own peril Gladstone's ideas on the relations between States. On British politics he has made a durable mark. Reverence for the good sense of ordinary men, a feeling for freedom as the best guarantee of genuine progress in society, the idea that public action must be morally justifiable: all these are now part of the common heritage of the great English parties, and it was Gladstone above all who made them so. He made them seem so necessary, indeed so inevitable, that nearly all of us now take them for granted.

Yet what has become of Gladstone's tool in the second half of his life for putting his political projects into execution—the Liberal party? To consider briefly its history since his death may help to reveal the extent to which it depended on his personality. We have seen how the project of Home Rule for Ireland, combined as it was with a negative attitude on Gladstone's part towards Chamberlain's projects of social reform; drove from the Liberal party most of its surviving Whig landowners and a small though noisy group of Radicals; and we have seen how little some of the men of eminence left in the party loved each other, so that Gladstone's last year as its leader was saddened by wrangles among those who disputed the succession to his place. These wrangles continued, and grew worse, after his death. He lived to see Chamberlain Colonial Secretary in a Conservative Cabinet, and he lived to see the Jameson Raid, but not its sequel when in 1899 war with the Boer republics was forced by strong public feeling on both sides, and by Milner's impetuosity, on which Chamberlain did not put a strong enough brake. During the war the Liberal party was divided, some holding that imperial expansion was a necessity of the times, or that in any case all patriots must support a war in which their country is engaged, others that patriotism is less important than justice, that the war was an unjust war fought for commercial motives, and that the duty of a Liberal must be to oppose it. The principal spokesman of this wing of the party, which had more support in the country than among the leaders, was Campbell-Bannerman. One of his phrases—'methods of barbarism', describing the camps in which Boer civilians were concentrated under insanitary conditions by British troops who had cleared them from their farms—was an inspiration to the Boers as well as to the British, and helped to secure the generous peace of 1902. There is little doubt which side Gladstone would have supported.

In 1902 the split in the Liberal party was narrowed in a controversy over education. Next year it was healed, unintentionally, by Chamberlain, who resigned and toured the country to campaign for a new Corn Law (by which he hoped to finance such Radical reforms as he could persuade his Conservative allies to accept). He was followed round England by Asquith, who deployed against him the armoury of Cobden's arguments with an intellectual adroitness matching Gladstone's own. Gladstone would have approved all that he said. When at the end of 1905 Campbell-Bannerman was called on to form a Government, Asquith's tact helped to adjust the party leaders' personal quarrels, and early in 1906 the Liberals, now united on a free trade policy, won a remarkable victory at a general election. The Unionists were much more heavily defeated than Gladstone had been in 1886; voting went decisively against them, and they saved only 157 seats. Under Campbell-Bannerman (who died in 1908) and Asquith, the Liberals were able to make genuine Liberal progress in every sphere but the Irish. The foundations of the 'welfare state' were laid when old age pensions were introduced in 1908 and a national insurance system in 1911. The condition of working men was much improved by several measures of the kind that Gladstone had favoured, though the growth of a parliamentary Labour party (founded in 1900) presented an eventual threat to the Liberals unless they could produce someone who could match Gladstone's hold over the imagination of the working classes and his appeal to their sense of justice.

The main Liberal achievement was the Parliament Act of 1911 which ended the Lords' powers to veto Liberal legislation, extensively employed in the previous five years and used finally, unwisely, and unconstitutionally, to reject a Budget. For this Act the authority of Gladstone's last speech in the Commons could be (and often was) quoted. The two general elections of 1910, fought on this issue, placed the Liberal party in dependence on the Irish party in the Commons, and in return for supporting the Parliament Act the Irish insisted on its use to pass Home Rule. A third Home Rule Bill was introduced in 1912, and passed the Commons three times, though the Lords always rejected it; under the Parliament Act it became law in 1914. It provided a federal solution of the problem, much on the lines on which Northern Ireland is governed today. The passage of this measure was opposed with extraordinary bitterness by the Unionists, and the Ulster complication became so serious that it brought Ireland right to the verge of civil war. Gladstone had under-estimated it when it was pressed in Parliament, and Asquith tried to ignore (as Gladstone would not have done) Ulster's insistence on freedom from Dublin, even when it was pressed in the streets of Belfast by Carson's private army of Ulster Volunteers. In 1914 an amending bill provided for the exclusion of the northern Irish counties for a limited time. By the time that these two bills became law (September 1914) the situation had entirely altered, for Great Britain had been at war for over a month.

Asquith's Foreign Secretary, Grey, worked on what he believed to be Gladstone's principles (he wrote once, on mature reflection, 'I have no doubt, taking force of character, energy, and intellectual power combined, that Gladstone was the greatest man in whose presence I have ever been'). The diplomatic catastrophe of 1914 was never within his control. In the winter of 1912–13 he had managed to avert a European war over a Balkan crisis, by an ambassadors' conference in London, the visible action of the Concert of Europe. He suggested the same remedy in the Balkan crisis of 1914, but the Central Powers were not prepared to apply it. Gladstone would certainly have approved the eventual decision of Asquith's Cabinet to honour a 75-year-old guarantee and declare war on Germany to defend the independence of Belgium—which Gladstone and Granville had taken pains to preserve in 1870.

The war was fatal to the Liberal party. An analyst of Gladstone's handwriting once noted that he 'would have made a good general or admiral—large power over practical detail'. Some of Asquith's colleagues possessed similar powers, but Asquith himself did not. He was too much a House of Commons man (Dilke had thought him a better parliamentarian even than Gladstone), too adept at finding formulæ for compromise, and too unpopular with the Unionist half of the nation, to command full confidence for the supreme conduct of a war that penetrated the daily lives of citizens as no previous war in British history had done. An intrigue removed him from power at the end of 1916, and the war was won under the political coalition of the Radical Lloyd George and the Unionist Milner (who had some robust Radicalism in him, but never had a chance to display it), supported by the rank Toryism of Bonar Law. Even worse from the Liberal party's point of view than the never-healed split between Asquith and Lloyd George was the demonstration that the war provided, through such bodies as the Allied Maritime Transport Council and the Ministry of Munitions, that socialism and a planned economy were not the idle dreams of theoreticians but practical realities. In the general election that followed the armistice at the end of 1918, Asquith's Liberal party did so badly that it had to abandon the front opposition bench to the Labour party, which had 63 members to its 33. Both were faced for four years by the overwhelming mass of the 526 supporters of Lloyd George's coalition with Bonar Law.

In Ireland, where a situation long tense had degenerated into civil war, this coalition attempted to enforce British rule by the lawless coercion of the Black and Tans, a body whose brutalities would have appalled Gladstone. In face of the manifest impossibility of repressing for ever the Irish national spirit, now thoroughly aroused, at the end of 1921 Lloyd George signed a treaty with the Irish rebel leaders from which the republic of Eire originated. Home Rule, long refused to argument, was thus in the end secured for a divided island by force.

The Labour party in Parliament has ever since 1918 remained larger than the Liberal, and has now definitely replaced the latter as the second of the two parties that the English electoral system demands. The Liberal attitude towards the Labour party's creed of socialism has always been hostile, on grounds of economic theory. Gladstone himself never gave serious consideration to the socialist case, and said in 1890 : 'For me socialism has no attractions : nothing but disappointment awaits the working classes if they yield to the exaggerated anticipations which are held out to them by the Labour party.' Such a view was natural for one brought up on the economists of his day; but would it have survived contact with the economic necessities of the present century or the aspirations of an educated working class, basing its claims on an appeal to justice that would strongly have attracted Gladstone, who always saw politics not as a separate subject but as a branch of morality?

It is time to turn from views of Gladstone's that did apply in past conditions, and can do so no longer because the conditions have changed, to those that did and do and will apply, for ever, to the political life of men.

Two points stand out as the central and critical doctrines of his political life : magnanimity among statesmen towards their opponents, and magnanimity among nations towards their fellow nations. Both these doctrines are indispensable for the continuance of an ordered and peaceful society, without violence, without persecution, with wit and critical tolerance instead of the dull intolerance of bigotry. Gladstone showed how relations between States will have to be conducted if the world is ever to shake itself free of its present troubles. In his day European affairs were set on their course by his greatest contemporary, Bismarck. Bismarck, the apologist of ruthlessness without moral scruple, thought that politics were concerned only with power. In an age of imperialist expansion and growing armaments he devised a European system centred on a powerful Prussian Germany, which lesser men proceeded after his fall, with reckless levity, to bring to disaster. Gladstone saw farther. He saw what the event proved, that no man is fit to be trusted with power uncontrolled by law; and as best he could, in a world disinclined to listen to him, he urged the cause of what he believed to be righteousness. In foreign as in home politics, he pointed to the necessary way. The choice remains open : Bismarck's way, the way of perpetual struggle, perpetual danger, and perpetual fear; or Gladstone's way, the recognition of law.

The gradual civilisation of passions in politics was one of Gladstone's chief studies, and it was a process which his own career has done much to further by the force of his splendid example. Acton—no mean judge—thought that, of all modern statesmen, 'in the three elements of greatness combined—the man, the power, and the result—character, genius, and success—none reached his level'. His example may help to keep alive the spirit of forbearance without which there is no progress in politics nor hope of peace, and to demonstrate the hollowness of the claims of the concentration camp and the ruthless 'dictatorship of the proletariat' to lead men towards a better organization of society.

Note on Books

TWO excellent books describe the general history of England during Gladstone's lifetime: E. Halévy's *History of the English People in the Nineteenth Century* (6 vols., trans., London,[1] 1924–51), and R. C. K. Ensor's *England 1870–1914* (Oxford, 1936). Halévy's work, unfortunately, is incomplete between 1841 and 1895. There are good bibliographies in Ensor's book and in E. L. Woodward's *The Age of Reform, 1815–1870* (Oxford, 1938).

A few useful fragments from Gladstone's letters have been published. Miss A. Ramm has edited (2 vols., 1952) his *Political Correspondence . . . [with] Granville* for 1868–76. D. C. Lathbury's *Correspondence on Church and Religion of W. E. Gladstone* (2 vols., 1910) provides commentary as well as texts. P. Guedalla edited *Gladstone and Palmerston* (1928) and *The Queen and Mr. Gladstone* (2 vols., 1933). A. Tilney Bassett, who has arranged with immense care the 750 volumes of Gladstone Papers in the British Museum, edited *Gladstone to his Wife* (1936), and earlier compiled a complete list of *Gladstone's Speeches*, with 14 texts, published in 1916. Fragments from Gladstone's letters are, of course, also scattered over scores of biographies of his contemporaries. His more interesting articles were republished by their author in *Glean-*

---

[1] All books are published in London unless otherwise stated.

ings of Past Years (7 vols., 1879) and *Later Gleanings* (1898).

There is no wholly satisfactory life of Gladstone. Morley's great *Life* (3 vols., 1903) is a splendid literary achievement, full of fascinating detail, written by a man who knew Gladstone well and who had served in two of his Cabinets, but not quite true in its perspectives. Of the numerous single-volume lives, three may be singled out: H. W. Paul's *Life of W. E. Gladstone* (1901) for local colour, G. T. Garratt *The Two Mr. Gladstones* (1936) for freshness of approach, and Dr. E. Eyck's *Gladstone* (trans., 1938) for comprehensiveness.

Two monographs cover particular aspects of Gladstone's career in detail: Dr. J. L. Hammond's *Gladstone and the Irish Nation* (1938), and Dr. R. W. Seton-Watson's *Disraeli, Gladstone, and the Eastern Question* (1935). Among slighter monographs may be mentioned Dr. P. Knaplund on *Gladstone and Britain's Imperial Policy* (1927), F. W. Hirst (who helped Morley with the *Life*) on *Gladstone as Financier and Economist* (1931), and W. E. Williams *The Rise of Gladstone, 1859–1868* (Cambridge, 1934).

The most vivid accounts of Gladstone are by members of his household, headed by his son, Herbert, Viscount Gladstone, with *After Thirty Years* (1928), a vigorous defence of his father's memory. There are two good accounts by his private secretaries: Sir E. W. Hamilton's *Mr. Gladstone* (1898) and Lord Kilbracken's *Reminiscences* (1931). Mrs. Drew's *Catherine Gladstone* (1919) and the *Diary* of Lady Frederick Cavendish (ed. J. Bailey, 2 vols., 1927) complete the domestic picture.

Table of Dates

G.E. = General Election.   P.M. = became Prime Minister.

Events concerning Gladstone in particular are in bold type.

1783 Pitt P.M.
1784 G.E. inaugurated 46 years of Tory majorities. Palmerston born
1788 Peel born
1789 French Revolution began
1793 Great Britain at war with France
1798 Irish Rebellion
1800 Act of Union with Ireland
1804 Disraeli born
1805 Battle of Trafalgar
1806 Pitt died
1809 **Gladstone born**
1812 Lord Liverpool P.M. Canning **M.P.** for Liverpool
1815 Bismarck born. Main Treaty of Vienna; Battle of Waterloo
1820 King George IV
1821 **Gladstone at Eton**
1822 Canning foreign secretary
1827 Canning P.M.; and died
1828 Wellington P.M. **Gladstone at Christ Church, Oxford**
1829 Catholic Relief Act
1830 Salisbury born. King William IV; G.E.; Grey P.M.
1831 Reform Bill defeated; G.E., Whig majority. **Gladstone's double first**

1832 Great Reform Bill passed; **G.E., Whig majority**

1833 **Gladstone entered Commons as M.P. for Newark**

1834 Melbourne P.M.; Peel P.M.; **Gladstone a junior minister under him**

1835 G.E., Conservative gains slight; Melbourne P.M.; **Gladstone resigned with Peel's Cabinet**

1836 Chamberlain born

1837 Queen Victoria; G.E., small Whig majority

1838 **Gladstone published** *Church and State*

1839 **Gladstone married**

1841 G.E., Conservative majority; Peel P.M.; **Gladstone Vice-President of Board of Trade**

1842 **Tariff revision**

1843 **Gladstone entered Cabinet as President, Board of Trade**

1845 **Gladstone resigned over Maynooth.** Irish Famine began

1846 **Gladstone Colonial Secretary.** Corn laws repealed, Conservatives split; Russell P.M.

1847 Ten Hours Act. G.E., no majority

1848 Revolutions in Europe. Public Health Act

1850 **Don Pacifico debate.** Peel died. **Gladstone in Naples**

1851 *Letters to Lord Aberdeen.* Palmerston dismissed

1852 Derby P.M.; G.E., no majority; Aberdeen P.M., **Gladstone his Chancellor of the Exchequer**

1853 **Gladstone's first budget.** Russo-Turkish War began

1854 Crimean War began

1855 Palmerston P.M. **Gladstone joined him, but resigned at once**

1856 Crimean War ended

1857 **China War debate**; G.E., Palmerston's victory; Indian Mutiny

1858 Orsini's plot; Derby P.M.; **Gladstone in Ionia.**

1859 G.E., Whig majority; Franco-Austrian War in Italy; Palmerston P.M. **with Gladstone at Exchequer**

1860 France annexed Savoy; **Cobden Treaty.** Italian unification began.

1861 U.S. civil war began. **Gladstone repealed paper duties**

1862 *Alabama* sailed. Bismarck P.M. of Prussia. **Gladstone supported American South**

1863 Polish Rebellion

1864. Danish war

1865 G.E., Palmerston's victory; Palmerston died; Russell P.M., **Gladstone leading Commons**

1866 **Reform Bill defeated.** German civil war. Derby P.M.

1867 Second Reform Act passed by Disraeli **under pressure from Gladstone and Bright**

1868 Disraeli P.M.; **G.E., Liberal majority; Gladstone P.M.**

1869 **Irish Church disestablished.** Suez Canal opened

1870 **Irish Land Act.** Education Act. Franco-Prussian War; **Gladstone protested about Alsace-Lorraine**

1871 Alsace-Lorraine annexed to Germany. British Army reformed

1872 Ballot Act. *Alabama* arbitration award

1873 **Gladstone resigned but had to resume office**

1874 **G.E., Conservative majority; Disraeli P.M.**

1875 **Gladstone retired from politics.** Disraeli bought Suez Canal shares

1876 *Bulgarian horrors* brought Gladstone back into politics

1877 Russo-Turkish War

1878 Congress and Treaty of Berlin

1879 Afghan and Zulu wars. **Midlothian campaign**

1880 **G.E., Liberal majority; Gladstone P.M.;** Turks left Dulcigno

1881 Majuba. Turks ceded Thessaly to Greece. Disraeli died. **Irish Land Act**; arrest of Parnell

1882 Parnell released; **Phœnix Park murders**; coercion. Egypt occupied

1883 Corrupt Practices Act

1884 Gordon sent to Sudan. **Third Reform Act**

1885 Gordon killed; Salisbury P.M.; Redistribution Act; G.E., no majority; *'Hawarden Kite'*

1886 **Gladstone P.M.; Liberals split; Home Rule Bill lost in Commons;** G.E., Conservative majority; Salisbury P.M.

1887 "Parnellism and crime" articles

1888 Local government reform

1889 Parnell commission report

1890 Bismarck dismissed. Parnell divorce case

1891 Newcastle programme. Parnell died

1892 G.E., small Liberal majority; **Gladstone P.M. for fourth time**

1893 **Second Home Rule Bill carried in Commons, defeated in Lords**

1894 **Gladstone resigned over naval estimates;** Rosebery P.M.

1895 Salisbury P.M.; G.E., Conservative majority (**Gladstone did not stand**). Jameson Raid

1896 **Gladstone's edition of Butler.** Armenian massacres; **Gladstone's last great speech, on them**

1898 **Gladstone died.**

Index

Aberdeen, 61–3, 65–70, 76, 166
Acton, 39, 41, 80, 177, 208
Adullamites, 100–1
Afghanistan, 122, 131–2, 165–6, 177
Alabama, 88, 114, 120, 123, 166, 198
Albert, Prince, 87
Alexandria, 158–9
Alsace-Lorraine, 71, 116–17, 184
Althorp (Spencer), 38, 44, 147
Arabi, 158–9
Argyll, 111, 142
Armenia, 122, 199–200
Army reform, 118–19, 152
Ashley, see Shaftesbury
Asquith, 190, 195, 203–6
Australia, 51, 100
Austria-Hungary, 78–9, 82–4, 92, 160, 184, 197

Balfour, 3, 155, 176, 187–8
Balkans, 69–70, 76, 128–30, 133, 205
Ballot, 118, 121, 123–4, 140, 152
Beaconsfield, see Disraeli
Belgium, 86, 116, 205
Benthamites, 3, 24–5, 32, 38–42
Bentinck, 53
Berlin, Congress of, 130, 138
Bismarck, 78, 91–4, 115–17, 160, 184, 197, 207–8
Black Sea, 70–1, 119
Board of Trade, 29, 45–8, 66
Boer wars, 150–2, 202
Boycott, 187 n.

Bradlaugh, 56, 136–7
Bright, J., 2, 70, 73, 86–7, 99–104, 122, 133, 135, 156, 159, 164, 172, 179, 182
Bruce (Aberdare), 118 n., 121–4
Bulgaria, 63, 69, 122, 128–30
Bunsen, 43
Burke, Edmund, 16, 21, 37 n., 57 n.
Burke, T. H., 147, 189
Butler, Bishop, 199

Cabinets, Gladstone's: *1868*, 106, 111, 116–18, 123; *1880*, 135, 139, 166; *1886*, 177–81; *1892*, 195–6, 198–9, 202
Campbell-Bannerman, 195, 202–3
Canning, 9–10, 16, 29, 34, 126–7
Cardwell, 111, 118
Carnarvon, 103, 149, 170–1, 194
Cavendish, Lord F., 147–8, 168, 180
Cavour, 67, 78, 82–4
Chamberlain, J., 2–3, 133, 146, 149, 153, 155, 170, 172–82, 191, 202–3; compared with Gladstone, 135, 178–9
Chartism, 4, 31, 35
Childers, 139
China, 73
Christ Church, Oxford, 14–19
Church and State, 37, 42–4, 49

Church of England, 20–5, 121, 172–3; see also Irish Church and Welsh Church

Churchill, Lord R., 56, 137, 166–7, 170–1, 183, 197 n., 201

Churchill, W. S., 197 n., 201

Civil Service, 118 and n.

Clarendon, 68, 73, 111, 114–15, 118 n.

Cobden, 2, 49, 70, 73, 85–7, 93–4, 97 n., 133, 197, 203

Coercion, Irish, 52, 107, 144–9, 166, 176, 187–8, 190, 206

Coleridge, S. T., 42

Colonial Office, 44, 50–1, 178, 202

Concert of Europe, 69, 74, 93, 115, 129, 138, 159–60, 205

Corn laws, 1, 35, 45–6, 49–53, 171, 203

Corrupt practices, 118, 121, 152–3, 155

Crimean War, 1, 30, 67–71, 93, 119, 132–3

Cyprus, 132, 138, 150, 161

Darwin, 3, 51

Davitt, 141–2, 145

Democracy, 35, 63, 99, 133, 150–2; and see Reform

Derby (Stanley), 1, 38, 45, 49, 50, 65, 68, 70, 76–7, 79, 90, 101, 103–4, 107

Derby stakes, 53, 199

Devonshire, see Hartington

Dilke, 3, 130, 133, 148, 175, 179, 205

Disraeli (Beaconsfield), 14, 31, 50, 52–3, 71–3, 77–9, 101–4, 106–8, 110, 112–13, 123–5, 128–34, 138–9, 141, 155–6, 158, 161, 167–9, 171, 186; compared with Gladstone, 3–4, 38, 90–5, 102

Dock labour, 48

Drink, 48, 124, 195

Education, 27, 31, 118, 121, 124, 172, 203

Egypt, 152, 157–64

Eton, 11–14

Europe, see Concert of Europe

Evangelicalism, 18–26

Factory Acts, 31–3, 122

Ferdinand II ('Bomba'), 60–3, 84, 91, 144

Finance, see Treasury

Finance bills, 96

Foreign policy, 114–15, 207–8; and see Alabama, Belgium, Bismarck, Concert of Europe, Egypt, France, Italy, Russia, or Turkey.

Forster, 121, 127, 144–7

Fowler, 195–6

Fox, C. J., 57 n., 97–8

France, 27–8, 39, 59, 63, 75, 78–9, 82–6, 92–4, 98, 157–60, 196–8

Franco-Prussian War, 13 n., 71, 115–17

Free trade, see Tariffs

French Treaty (1860), 85–6

Garibaldi, 79, 82–3

General elections, 172; 1832, 37; 1835, 44; 1841, 44; 1847, 53; 1852, 65; 1857, 73, 133; 1859, 78; 1865, 100; 1868, 104, 121; 1874, 123–5; 1880, 131–6; 1885, 137, 170, 172–3, 182 n.; 1886, 183–6, 203; 1892, 195; 1895, 199 and n.; 1906, 203; 1910, 204; 1918, 206

Gladstone, Catherine (wife), 4, 60, 85, 89 n., 108, 147, 154, 166, 174

Gladstone, Helen (sister), 10

Gladstone, Herbert (son), 174–5, 210
Gladstone, Sir John (father), 6–10, 13 n., 20–1, 37, 45
Gladstone, Thomas (grandfather), 6
Gladstone, W. E., character, 1–5, 10–11, 17–18, 67, 73, 122, 174, 179, 186, 207–8
Gordon, 162–5, 178
Goschen, 97, 117, 138, 172
Granville, 81, 115–17, 119–20, 126, 134, 137–8, 160, 165–6, 177–8, 180, 195, 205, 209
Graham, 35, 45, 54, 65, 67, 79, 95
Greece, 12, 35, 59–60, 69, 128, 138
Greenwich, 123 n.
Greville, 49, 67, 85
Grey, Earl, 30, 37, 44
Grey, Sir Edward, 205

Hallam, 12–15
Harcourt, 96, 102, 180–1, 195, 198
Hartington (Devonshire), 127, 134, 154, 162, 177, 179–81, 196
Hawarden, 54, 71, 126, 156, 162, 174–5
Home Rule, 108, 140, Ch. XII, 187–94, 201–2, 206; first Home Rule bill, 181–2; second Home Rule bill, 196, 201; third Home Rule bill, 204
Homer, 12, 71, 128, 199, 201
Huskisson, 19, 29

Imperial policy, Disraeli's, 4, 131, 138–9, 158; Gladstone's, 56–9, 161
Income tax, 34, 45, 67, 108, 123

India, 77, 131–2, 158, 165, 167
International law, 119–21
'Invincibles', 147–8
Ionia, 77–8
Ireland, 3, 15, 29, 106–14, 122, 127, 139–49, 152, 157, Ch. XII, 191, 193–4, 206; and see Coercion, Home Rule
Irish Church, 24, 37, 43, 108, 110–11, 118
Irish crime, see Coercion
Irish famine, 49, 109
Irish land, 16, 108–13, 118 and n., 142–8, 187 and n.
Irish Nationalist party, 124, 127, 140–1, 157, 167–8, 170, 173, 176–9, 184, 189–90, 193–4
Irish universities, 48, 112, 123
Italy, 2, 23, 60–3, 75, 78–84, 86, 102, 197

Kilmainham, 145–6

Labour party, 201, 203, 205–7
Lancashire, 89, 98, 123 n., 141
Law, A. Bonar, 205–6
Law reform, 29, 31, 75, 97
Licensing, 124, 195
Lincoln, Abraham, 86, 88
Lincoln, Lord, 15
Liverpool, 6–7, 13 n., 88, 173, 199
Lloyd George, 96, 198 n., 205–6
Local government, 28, 31, 135, 172, 179, 195–6
Lords, House of, 16, 45, 50, 95–6, 104, 113, 142–3, 155–6, 168–9, 175, 178, 196–7, 203–4
Lowe (Sherbrooke), 51, 100, 111, 123, 127–8
Lyons, 87, 115

Maamtrasna, 148–9
Macaulay, 28, 43
Mahdi, 161–4
Majuba, 150–2
Manning, 26 n., 110
Masterman, 50 n.
Marx, 4, 33
Maynooth, 48–9, 112
Mazzini, 63, 153
Melbourne, 30, 44
Metaphysical Society, 128
Midlothian, 131–4, 166, 173–4, 185, 195
Mill, J. S., 3, 24–5, 39, 41–2, 76, 104, 109
Milner, 198, 202, 206
Mitchelstown, 188
Morley, 3, 102, 181, 188–9, 192, 195, 210; and quoted *passim*

Naples, 60–3, 91, 107 n., 128
Napoleon I, 28–9, 67, 92
Napoleon III, 31, 67, 75–6, 78–85, 89–90, 92–4, 115–16
National Liberal Federation, 133, 186
Newark, 15, 37, 50
Newcastle, Duke of, 15, 37, 50
Newcastle Programme, 195–7
Northampton, 136
Northcote (Iddesleigh), 95, 132, 137, 156–7

Obstruction, 119 and n., 140–1, 144, 189–90
Orsini, 75
O'Shea, 146, 170, 182 n., 191–2
O'Shea, Katharine, 146, 191–2
Oxford, 14–19, 23, 51, 94, 123 n.
Oxford Movement, 11, 23–6, 43

Pacifico, 59–60
Palmerston, 2, 47 n., 60–4,

Chs. VI and VII, 120, 130, 133, 138, 149, 194, 198
Paper Duties, 95–6
Parliament Act (1911), 96, 178, 196, 203–4
Parliamentary committees, 33
Parliamentary procedure, see Obstruction
Parnell, 8, 141–7, 157, 169–70, 176–7, 179, 182 and n., 187–94
Peel, 1, 8, 15, 29–30, 34–5, 43–53, 60, 65, 104, 126, 137, 171, 186; compared with Gladstone, 14, 38, 117, 185; with Pitt, 51
Penjdeh, 165–6, 177
Phœnix Park, 147–8, 168, 180, 189
Piggott, 189–90
Pitt (the younger), 32, 51, 66, 194
Pluralism, 22
Poor Law, 31
Prostitution, 153–5

Radicals, 119, 121, 124, 133, 135–6, 149, 152–7, 164, 172, 186, 195, 203
Redmond, 194
Reform: general, 28–35, 81, 97, 106, 178; Parliamentary, 51, 78, 95, 98–101, 118, and see Ballot; *1832*, 15–16, 29–30, 34; *1867*, 101–4, 118, 121, 133, 168, 171; *1884*, 152, 155–7
Roman Catholics, 10, 15, 23, 26 n., 29, 55–6, 65, 127, 168
Rosebery, 131, 156, 169, 177–8, 195, 199
Russell, 30, 49, 54–5, 59, 63–5, 67–8, 76, 79–88, 90–2, 97, 100–1, 106, 186
Russia, 67–71, 76, 119, 130–3, 160, 165–6, 197–8

Salisbury, 11, 52, 76, 98, 103, 156–7, 167, 170–6, 185, 187–9, 195, 197
Schnadhorst, 186
Shaftesbury (Ashley), 11, 18, 26 n., 32–3, 122, 167
Shelley, 12, 17
Slavery, 7–9, 37–8, 86–9, 161, 163 n.
Slesvig-Holstein, 91–2, 157
Socialism, 205–7
'Society', 4, 29, 63, 66, 134, 152, 169, 194
South Africa, 131, 150–2, 202
Speakers, 101, 102, 136, 137, 144
Spencer, 147–9, 171, 177, 198–9
Stanley, see Derby
Stansfeld, 153–4
Sudan, 161–4
Suez Canal, 74, 157–8

Tariffs, 29, 34, 45–6, 59, 66, 95, 113, 203; and see Corn Laws
Times, The, 3, 31, 71, 85, 99, 113, 116; and Parnell, 189–91
Tocqueville, A. de, 55–7
Trade Unions, 2, 98, 121–4, 139–40, 188
Treasury, 34, 66–7, 123, 139, 147, 160, 181

Trent, 87
Trevelyan, G. O., 149
Turkey, Chs. VI and IX, 138, 158, 199–200

Ulster, 180, 187 n., 204
U.S.A., 86–91, 98, 113–14, 120–1, 123, 141
Utilitarianism, see Benthamites

Victor Emmanuel II, 67, 82
Victoria, Queen, 50, 66, 68, 81, 95, 106, 112, 117–20, 123, 134–5, 138, 154, 156, 162, 169, 177–8, 180, 183, 194, 196, 199

Wellington, 15, 49–50, 68, 168
Welsh Church, 47, 118 n., 195, 199
West Indies, 7–9, 37 and n.
Whigs, 4, 30–1, 66, 79, 111, 134, 136, 157, 173, 177, 180, 186, 202
Wilhelm I and II, 115
William IV, 38, 44
Wolseley, 159, 163–4
Working classes, 27–35, 48, 66, 85, 97–105, 121–4, 139–40, 152, 185, 188, 203–4, 207

Zululand, 131, 150